"In *Big Enough*, Lee LeFever uses his finely honed explainer skills to provide a refreshing, personal guide to designing a business around the values that matter most to you. *Big Enough* offers plenty of tactics and tips, but more importantly it gives readers a chance to rethink their definitions of success and adjust their working lives accordingly. As the sole proprietor of a Big Enough business myself, I found a lot to steal here, and I think you will, too."

AUSTIN KLEON, *New York Times*–bestselling author of *Steal Like an Artist*

"We often hear about how the internet has allowed companies to get big fast, but the same forces can provide great leverage for individuals or small partnerships to choose different success metrics, like freedom, health, or satisfaction. In *Big Enough*, Lee LeFever shares the approach he and his wife took in building their small online business, and the incredible flexibility it's given them in how they live. As the owner of a tiny online business, I wish I'd had this thoughtful and engaging book as a blueprint when I started out."

JASON KOTTKE

"This book redefines sustainability for entrepreneurs. If you've ever wondered how much is enough, this book will guide you to your answer. Lee LeFever is gentle, helpful, optimistic, and kind—exactly what you'd never expect from a successful tech entrepreneur."

JESSICA HAGY, author of *How to Be Interesting*

"*Big Enough* sits at the intersection of creativity, entrepreneurship, and a high-quality, well-lived life. Read this book as a roadmap to turning your creative dreams into your career."

CHASE JARVIS, photographer and founder of CreativeLive

"There's a massive gap between the fantasy of running your own company and the real-world experience required to start something that you can carry forth into being a company that's Big Enough to support your lifestyle without overtaking your entire universe. Lee LeFever shows you how to move from fantasy to reality."

CHRIS BROGAN, founder of StoryLeader™

"A practical business autobiography, approachable and useful ... Lee LeFever helps you understand the real difference between freelancing and entrepreneurship (and what to do about it)."

SETH GODIN, founder of Akimbo.com

"*Big Enough* is not just another story about being a successful entrepreneur; it's a guide for how to design a successful business by focusing on your desired lifestyle and your values. I only wish I'd read this book earlier."

NICOLE HERZOG, Swiss tech investor and entrepreneur

"There is a growing movement of smart business owners who are more concerned with 'enough' than the typical 'more.' Lee LeFever tells his story of letting personal values and freedom chart his course in business, to help others determine how they want to define their own success."

PAUL JARVIS, author of *Company of One*

"I've admired the work that Lee and Sachi LeFever have done with Common Craft over the years. I loved reading the stories behind their success. They made it look easy... of course, reality is always a little trickier. This book was fun to read, incredibly open and honest, and came at such a perfect time for me! I learned so much from Lee's insights into building a Big Enough business and it really inspired me to rethink a lot of what I'm working on. If you are an entrepreneur with heart, you'll love this book."

TARA HUNT, author, researcher, and founder, Phlywheel

"Big Enough is a refreshing look at the types of businesses and lives we can build when we stop focusing on growth for growth's sake. Lee and Sachi LeFever have built a great business in a way that has enabled a fulfilling and flourishing lifestyle. We can learn a lot from how they optimized their time and their projects, and relentlessly focused on the opportunities that align with their values."

CHRIS SAVAGE, co-founder and CEO of Wistia

"Lee LeFever takes you behind the scenes as he and his wife build a Big Enough business that defies the default, often destructive ambitions of going big or going home. This book is filled with honest, practical, and inspiring tips for building a business. *Big Enough* shows you how work can add meaning and fulfillment to your life instead of draining it away."

BUSTER BENSON, author of *Why Are We Yelling?* and co-founder of 750words.com

BIG ENOUGH

Lee LeFever

ENOUGH

Building a
Business That
Scales with
Your Lifestyle

● PAGE
● TWO
BOOKS

Cataloguing in publication information is available
from Library and Archives Canada.

ISBN 978-1-989603-18-5 (paperback)
ISBN 978-1-989603-19-2 (ebook)

Page Two
www.pagetwo.com

Edited by Amanda Lewis
Copyedited by Taisha Garby
Proofread by Alison Strobel
Cover design by Peter Cocking
Interior design by Fiona Lee
Printed and bound in Canada by Friesens
Distributed in Canada by Raincoast Books
Distributed in the US and internationally
by Publishers Group West, a division of Ingram

20 21 22 23 24   5 4 3 2 1

www.leelefever.com

For Dolores

Contents

Prologue: The Scale of You *xiii*

1   **More Hours, More Money** *1*

2   **Return on Luck** *13*

3   **Work for Hire** *23*

4   **Choice as a Shareholder Value** *37*

5   **The Business of Permission** *45*

6   **Designing for the Future** *55*

7   **A Platform of One's Own** *63*

8   **Live the Monetorium** *77*

9   **Turning Copycats into Customers** *93*

10   **Success through Failure** *105*

11   **The Power Not to Care** *119*

Conclusion: Big Satisfaction on a Small Island *127*

Epilogue: Defining "Big Enough" for Yourself *139*

Acknowledgments *147*

Notes *149*

Prologue

The Scale of You

HAD BEEN DREAMING about this moment since the first time I visited the Pacific Northwest, in college. I was sitting in my truck, about to drive 3,000 miles from Charleston, South Carolina, to Seattle, Washington, where I would start a new life.

I had completed a master's in health administration and my goal was to find a job in healthcare technology. I had entrepreneurial dreams and knew that someday I'd own my own company. But at age twenty-five, I also knew I needed to put in my time as an employee.

It was 1998, and the rise of the internet made everything feel possible.

Seattle seemed like an innovation hub and I wanted to be in the middle of it. I knew that if I got my foot in the door, I could begin a new phase of my life, build connections, and eventually start my own business.

As I sat in the parking lot of my apartment building in Charleston, the enormity of the moment was not lost on me. The U-Haul trailer attached to my truck was full of nearly everything I owned. I took a deep breath, started the engine, and began backing out of the parking space. When I heard the wrenching sound of bending metal, I immediately knew what had happened. In my distracted state, I wasn't thinking about the trailer, which now sat perpendicular to the truck in jack-knife formation. I jumped out to see the damage my carelessness had wrought and found a bumper bent to a worrying degree. It was not an auspicious start to the journey.

A couple of days later, I was on my way to the west coast with a new bumper. After a few months of networking, I found a job as a data analyst at a healthcare data company and began to settle into life in Seattle. My career and path to being an entrepreneur started in a tiny cubicle on the eighth floor of a high-rise.

At the time, I was seduced by the stories of young entrepreneurs who founded businesses that grew to have thousands of employees, and offices around the world. I wanted, someday, to appear in the pages of a magazine like *Fast Company* or *Entrepreneur*, the ultimate validation and marker that showed my company had made it. With the income from being a successful founder, I could live the good life and have the freedom to decide what lifestyle I wanted.

This dream might sound familiar. Most people who are interested in entrepreneurship see it as a path out of debt and dependence. With enough money, conventional thinking tells us, life could be fundamentally better. I was not immune to this perspective. In starting a business, I saw a way to be independent and earn an income that could afford a comfortable lifestyle. If I got lucky, I could become rich and have ultimate freedom.

Today, I'm older, slightly wiser, and considerably better at backing up trailers. I've come to understand that it's possible for business success to create life-changing wealth, but it's rare. And often, the stories portrayed in *Fast Company* (or today more often on podcasts and YouTube) present a romantic notion that conveniently leaves out the day-to-day realities of owning and running a business. We're led to believe that outside the walls of corporate jobs, fame, fortune, and a life of happiness await those who are ready to accept the challenge.

The problem is that this version of entrepreneurship can become a trap. Talented people dream of starting a company that offers them the opportunity to earn a living based on their skills and passions. By owning a business, they can finally be independent and free to work on what matters to them. The trap appears when a business becomes successful and suddenly, they're filling the role of a manager, bookkeeper, or salesperson. Their success has come at an unexpected cost.

While some may be happy running a business that aims to be stable to growing, many entrepreneurs dream of unicorn success and long for the day when they can sell their business, profiting themselves and their stakeholders. The allure is undeniable, and for a lucky few, it happens—a big exit from the business pays for their years of toil. And good for them.

But the stark reality of entrepreneurship is it's inherently risky and can make life a struggle. Even owners of profitable businesses find themselves stuck—they can pay the bills, but not retire. Or their business becomes too big to evolve, or there isn't a buyer interested in their model. Sometimes, the exit ramps don't appear.

In reality, owning a business can be a long and rigorous grind, and the grind takes a toll. Business success often comes with a growing list of commitments that eat away at lifestyle, happiness, and health. Visions of independence and wealth are replaced with long hours, endless meetings, volumes of email, hustling for new clients, and feelings of obligation to investors and boards. The hours in each day are consistently filled. True vacations and downtime become rare. And weekends? What's a weekend? Hiring and managing employees takes incredible dedication. Personal lives suffer. And did I mention all the meetings?

This sort of professional life is now the norm. Entrepreneurs keep the dream in sight, value the drive, and sacrifice time and lifestyle today for the potential of more tomorrow. It can seem that landing the next big client, winning an award, or reaching a desired revenue will unlock the potential to sell the company or retire comfortably. For many entrepreneurs, this goal always seems just out of reach.

I certainly don't wish to denigrate entrepreneurial pursuits. We need more people to take risks and push through to create great companies and products. Many of these people are my heroes. My point is that entrepreneurship takes many forms and produces numerous outcomes, some of which are not traditional measures of success.

Having lived in Seattle for over twenty years, I've seen many friends devote their lives to building high-growth start-ups. They put in 80+ hours a week for years, in part, because they see an opportunity for a life-changing exit in the form of their company selling for tens of millions of dollars. Maybe even billions. Their version of entrepreneurship is high risk and high reward. Some have seen success, some are still waiting, and many have moved on.

Because these kinds of start-ups make the news, it's easy to assume they represent the ultimate form of business with the ultimate outcome: enough money to retire and circle the world on a mega-yacht, or buy a tropical island. When everyone is chasing unicorns, it can start to feel that doing it "right" means trading your life and your wellness for a shot at the big time. Carpe diem. After all, it's only your life.

What I've realized is that the dreams I had of developing a start-up, being written about in magazines, and counting my fabulous riches were, ultimately, not healthy or productive for me. Over time, I realized that my real dream was building and running a business that suits the person I am and the life I want to lead. I don't need an ipo or huge exit for validation.

I've found that there are few rules when it comes to objectively evaluating success in business. To me, success comes from running a business that matches the person you are, or want to become. By connecting your values to your business, you can create the lifestyle and level of satisfaction that works for you.

Over a decade ago, my wife, Sachi, and I set out to test what was possible in life and work. Our dream was to develop our company, Common Craft, into a reflection of who we are. We discovered a healthier approach to business that's focused on being lightweight and agile, with the potential to scale easily. For us, that's success.

Our story is unique, but the lessons are universal. At its heart, Common Craft is a projection of us. I want you to keep that in mind as you read because you are an individual with your *own* values and skills. You are not a conduit to make a venture capitalist wealthier or a cog in a lifeless machine. You have a choice in how your business impacts your life.

Your path to success may be different from ours, and that's the point. What matters is the intention to think ahead and design a business that works for you and the life you want to lead. Like us, you might find there is beauty and value in building a business that's "Big Enough."

1

More Hours,
More Money

IN THE SPRING of 2003, I sat down with a few official forms and started the process to legally create Common Craft, the company that has employed me ever since. I had quit my job only weeks before and Common Craft would be my one-person consulting company. Within a few weeks, a certificate arrived in the mail that said it was official. Common Craft was a licensed business in the state of Washington and the city of Seattle and as such, I owed them part of my business's income. It was literally the first of many costs of doing business.

The fact that I had no customers, no income, no employees, and no experience running a business didn't matter. Just after launching the company, I asked Sachi's father, an entrepreneur himself, for his permission to marry her. He kindly obliged and expressed his confidence that I was on my way to making Common Craft a real company. His and his daughter's faith in me helped soothe my anxiety.

That faith, to some degree, came from a sense of momentum that I felt too. Leading up to quitting my job, I had created an online community program at the healthcare data company where Sachi and I met. I was the online community manager between 1999 and 2003 and discovered a career that was a near-perfect fit with my passion for communication.

Being the first online community manager in the company came with an opportunity to practice the skill of explanation. The idea of an online community of customers was new to most people in the company, and in the early days, I spent a lot of time explaining what an online community is and why the company needed to have one. I knew the company needed to get ahead of the curve and start seeing their community of customers as a valuable resource. I was an evangelist for this early form of social media and loved the challenge of helping someone appreciate the potential of what I saw and understand it clearly.

After over three years in the community manager position, it became clear that I didn't have a lot of options for advancing. Every career path at the company led me away from being the community manager, and that was the only job I wanted. At the same time, I was convinced that online communities were going to be huge and I had the potential to become an expert in the field. I wanted to start a company that could be my vehicle for earning a living based on my passion and skills. So, I quit my job, started Common Craft, and took what seemed like the most obvious path to income: consulting.

Sachi was my biggest champion. Through months of prodding and cajoling, she'd convinced me that the time was right to quit. She planned to keep her job so we'd both have income and health insurance. One day, we hoped Common

Craft would pay the bills, but for a while, the income was as imaginary as the business.

What was real were all the details of forming Common Craft and creating processes to manage it. Was it going to be an LLC or a Corporation? Did I need a bookkeeper? What about a consulting contract? Did I need a lawyer? Could I do my taxes myself? All those details seemed to matter so much at the time, but looking back I can see that I really wanted to feel productive and moving forward. This busywork gave me a sense of purpose in the absence of customers.

In those first few months of Common Craft, I sprang from bed each morning with a sense that I was on my way. My office was a spare bedroom with an IKEA desk and laptop computer. In terms of capital investments, those items and our internet connection were all it took.

The bigger investment was an emotional one. I had to learn to become my own boss. Day after day, Sachi went to her job as a project manager and left me with the house to myself. In the beginning, I didn't have clients to keep me engaged, so the potential to goof off was very real. What saved me was the Common Craft blog, which became my focus. Every day, I blogged about online communities and anything that interested me. I felt like I was practicing what I was preaching, and soon, everyone would have a blog. It felt like I was living in the future.

Through the blog, my goal was to build visibility and credibility. I was passionate about social media and wanted more than anything to help others see its potential. From my perspective, wikis, blogs, and social networks were usually free, powerful, easy to use, and had the potential to become mainstream—and I wanted to help make these new tools and ideas easy to understand. This focus on communication is what inspired the name of the company. Communication, to me, is the most "common craft" and one that people take for granted.

The problem I saw was a lack of clear communication. At the time, these tools weren't being adopted because no one was explaining them clearly. Articles and websites tended to focus on features and specifications, instead of explaining why any normal person should care about a wiki or a blog. Put simply, I wanted to help everyday people care about what was becoming social media.

I started writing blog posts with the stated goal of explanation. These were posts like "RSS Described in Plain English" and "Wikis Described in Plain English." Up to that point, most of my blogging was based on articles I wanted to share or quotes from other bloggers. These new posts were different—there was something about the process of explaining technology that felt like home. Before long, a bit of traffic started to flow to commoncraft.com and I saw it as an indication that there was a need for this kind of writing.

My consistent blogging in the earliest days of Common Craft was financially unproductive, but jump-started the brand, brought in modest traffic, and, above all, provided an outlet and a way to feel I was being productive. With Sachi earning a solid living, I didn't feel immense pressure to support us. We both knew that starting a business takes time and neither of us planned for Common Craft to make a real financial contribution for many months. Plus, not only was I starting a new company, I was doing it in a nascent industry.

I balanced all my passion and expertise with a real fear that I didn't know how to be an effective consultant. I had expertise and a blog, but no experience working with clients. I didn't know how to put together a proposal or price my services. I didn't know what my clients would expect of me or what deliverables I could produce. I read a few books that helped a little, but what kept me up at night was this worry that I'd get hired and then realize I wasn't up to the task. I had no proven processes or models to follow like the ones I imagined "real" professional consultants having. I was just a guy with experience in an emerging field, and a lot of passion.

Thankfully, over time, some interest in my services started to build. Emails began to arrive from organizations that were starting online communities and needed help. I learned about their needs and wrote proposals. I tracked each hour I worked on a project and every month, sent them a bill for my services. I was finally in business and it was so gratifying to have a check arrive addressed to "Common Craft, LLC." Little Common Craft was earning modest revenue and over time, I grew more comfortable with the process of working with clients.

When I look back at that version of Common Craft, I can see that fee-for-service is a relatively simple and common way to earn a living. I was essentially a freelancer who was paid by the hour. I was converting labor (my time and effort) into capital (income) in the form of a service. But at the time, it never occurred to me that I had a business model, or why that mattered. I was doing what it took to earn a living in the most direct path possible, which is probably the case for most businesses. They start and grow as a way to put food on the table or to address a need in the marketplace, not to follow a business model.

My consulting practice was not that different from businesses you work with every day. Whether it's a local landscaper or a hairdresser, the business is based on what that person does well, and the customers who pay for that expertise. Recently, I saw a perfect example. I asked a local arborist named Justin to come to our property to evaluate our trees. The moment he arrived, it was clear he was in the right job. He described trees with awe and fascination. You could imagine him as a kid, climbing every tree he could find. He's fortunate to have a business that enables him to pursue his passion. The value of Justin's company resides in him, his skills, and the hours he puts into the work.

These kinds of businesses are often referred to as "lifestyle" businesses because their version of entrepreneurship enables a simpler lifestyle than running a growing company. They are not focused on exponential growth, fabulous riches, or outlandish business strategies. Their owners are happy scooping ice cream, creating art, consulting, or writing from home. They're independent and supporting themselves, maybe a family, or a few employees.

Common Craft, for a few years, was a lifestyle business. I loved being a one-person company and having the freedom to make my own hours and be my own boss. But over time, as I acquired more consulting clients, I felt the need to think bigger. Unless I grew my business, how was I going to appear in a magazine and earn the respect of my peers? Social media continued to gain in popularity and I started to see that Common Craft had the potential to take on more clients and become a different kind of company.

As a service-based business, hiring was my only viable path to growth. To make more income, Common Craft needed more consulting hours and those would come with more consultants. When human effort is attached to income, growth requires more humans. Every service-based business, from solo freelancers to small family businesses to global firms, is subject to this constraint. More people = more hours = more income. For many business owners, hiring happens in relation to demand. A new hire comes onboard to relieve the stress and help the company earn more income. It's a logical approach to supporting a growing service business and one that usually comes without forethought. Hiring is often a given. The problem, from my perspective, is that once a company crosses the employee Rubicon, it begins operating in a new context that can come as a shock to business owners.

Let's say I wanted to increase Common Craft's income and I was already working fifty hours a week. What could I do? I could raise my rates and reduce expenses, and that would be helpful, but not make a significant difference (there's only so much you can raise your rates, based on service offering and market demand). As a one-person service, Common Craft's income would quickly reach a ceiling connected to the amount of hours I worked.

So, I would need to hire more consultants, but it's not that simple. With employees come all sorts of issues that change the business. The new consultants need to be trained and paid and managed. They need equipment and vacations, maybe office space and benefits. What started as a lifestyle business becomes something different, and in this evolution, I'd become a manager. Suddenly people would be dependent on my company for their livelihood. Keeping these newly hired consultants busy, in the form of additional clients, would be my main job. Was I really prepared to be a salesperson?

No matter how many employees I hired, I'd still be playing the same game because everything is based on billable hours and humans can only work so much in a day. As the income ceiling gets higher, so do expenses. This difference between income and expenses, the margin, is limited in service businesses. Of course, this connection between human effort and income has not prevented a wide variety of service companies from becoming global success stories. KPMG, Deloitte, and Accenture are consulting firms that are mostly services. Design and engineering firms like IDEO and frog are based on services. Marketing, advertising, and PR firms are mostly services. Bookkeepers, law firms, construction companies... the list is long and illustrious. My point is not that services don't work as a business. They can be incredibly successful. But like every business model, a service business comes with limitations and trade-offs.

As a young consultant, none of this was on my mind. From 2003 to 2006, I continued to build an audience through the Common Craft blog and had a few long-term consulting engagements that kept the lights on. I was content not working in a cubicle, but I wanted more than consulting and hourly pay. I was searching for something that would take Common Craft in new directions—whatever those were. My perspective on business models started to change thanks to the Common Craft blog. I created a few far-flung relationships with people who enjoyed chatting about my recent posts. One of my readers in the UK, Tim, was an experienced businessperson. As a follow-up to one of my posts about my consulting, he wrote to say that I needed to "productize" my business. I knew what he meant, but I had no idea how to make it happen. At the time, I saw making products as a marketing strategy. I could sell my expertise via a nice package of services with a specific price. That's a product, right?

Looking back, I see that I wasn't thinking about the real differences between offering a product and performing a service. While it seemed like a detail at the time, I now consider the difference between products and services to be one of the defining factors of entrepreneurship. Clearly understanding the difference is key to thinking about business opportunities, how companies grow, and the consequences of that growth.

A service business ties human labor to income. Humans embody the value. More haircuts, more money. A product business breaks that connection. Human labor is still necessary, but it is not tied directly to income. Instead, people work to create a product that becomes the business's source of income. The product embodies the value and is often regarded as intellectual property (IP). A patent, for example, can ensure that a company's invention is unique in the market. And unlike consulting hours, a product can scale. It helps, too, that products don't take vacations or come down with the flu.

When income isn't based on human effort, it can grow more quickly and often with fewer headaches. A small team can produce a product that has the potential to reach a global audience and grow income exponentially. Because overhead and expenses aren't as connected to people, margins can be much higher. But like any business model, there are significant trade-offs.

Putting a product into the world, whether it's an app for a phone, or the phone itself, requires an upfront investment. Products, unlike people, must be designed, developed, tested, produced, distributed, and supported. In most cases, the biggest investments happen before the product hits the market. That's the risk. You could spend years of your life and millions of dollars creating a product only to find out that no one wants to buy it or that the market had changed. Sadly, this is a common outcome—think of how many apps are launched each year, and how many fail.

Another factor is skillset. Small service-based businesses are often successful because the people doing the work are passionate about it, like Justin the arborist. They've put in years of effort to hone their craft. A product business often requires the owner to have a skillset that's more focused on managing and growing the business. Unlike most services, products often have to compete in a competitive marketplace where being first or fabulous is practically a requirement for success. To pull it off, people who run successful product-based companies may need to have a real passion for both the product and for solving business problems, like marketing, engineering, manufacturing, and distribution.

Despite the risks and requirements, many entrepreneurs love product businesses because of the potential rewards. A low-stakes investment could create a product that people love. This product could endure, or require upgrades over time, leading to repeat business. Because income from the product isn't tied to the effort of individuals, it can scale easily and produce generous profit margins. Since there is a clear value, growth potential, and IP, this type of business can be sold for millions and allow a comfortable retirement. This scenario isn't as likely with a service business because the value is tied to people and associated expenses. It's clear why this model attracts entrepreneurs who are tired of service businesses and ready to take the risk and put everything into making it happen. But not everyone is a candidate for this type of lifestyle.

When I was a consultant, creating a product seemed out of reach. I wasn't a software developer, industrial designer, or engineer who had the skills to create a product. I didn't have the capital or connections to invest in an idea. But more than that, I was comfortable in the quiet confines of my home office. I could handle my small client list and was proud of the work I was performing. As I established my business, I realized that as much as I admired high-flying entrepreneurs and wanted to become one eventually, the path to making that happen wasn't obvious.

That perspective started to change in 2007. Thanks to a bit of luck and an experiment in making media, Sachi and I came to understand that new kinds of businesses were possible. Through years of experimentation, hard work, and an acceptance of risk, we eventually found that it's possible to design a business that operates somewhere between a Mom and Pop service business and a global product company. And in that middle ground are new opportunities to focus on business success alongside lifestyle goals. Selling digital products to a small group of dedicated fans or customers offers the chance to earn a good living and live a satisfying life. Using e-commerce tools, a home-based business can serve a global market without employees. In some cases, that business can be designed to produce income on a passive basis, providing the owners with time to put back into the business or into whatever makes them happy.

Over many years, we saw how conventional perceptions of success worked against business owners. Instead of the good life, a growing business often created drag, dependency, and fewer choices. We took a different path that led to greater autonomy and more choices.

Ours is not a story you'd read about in *Fast Company*, but I'm prouder of it than anything I might have created that landed me on the cover of a magazine. It's a modest story of two people working from home trying to figure out how to optimize their business for the lives they wanted to lead. This book tells that story, and explains why this form of business is possible and represents a saner, healthier approach to entrepreneurship.

THE TAKE HOMES:

→ Quitting your job and starting a business can be stressful. Find an outlet that keeps you engaged in your work, even if it doesn't produce direct income. Productivity can take many forms, including blogging, podcasting, or creating videos.

→ If possible, ask for help in starting your business. In the US, for instance, a spouse or partner may be able to provide health insurance. A friend or family member may be able to help with your initial expenses or even offer a used office desk. A bank may be able to loan you enough to get you through the first few months.

→ Your chances of success increase significantly when you are passionate about your work. Pay attention to what gets you excited and engaged. Is there a subject you can't stop talking about?

→ Keep your options open and understand business model basics. You may start with services, and then see the potential of products. Try to remain flexible enough to evolve and avoid traps.

→ The chances of striking it rich are very small. Your time may be better spent focusing on what you value in life, and how your business can support that lifestyle.

Return on Luck

EVERY ENTREPRENEUR HAS ideas. Once the entrepreneurial juices start flowing, everything starts to look like an opportunity destined for success. It's part of what attracts people to start businesses. The reality is that most business ideas don't survive their first contact with the real world.

There is a big difference between having ideas and turning them into successful businesses. For most entrepreneurs, the process starts with a spark that turns into a flame and then a fire. How that spark happens isn't the same for everyone and in many cases, it can come down to luck. They are in the right place at the right time. They strike up a conversation with someone on a plane, they make a fortuitous mistake, they notice a detail that was overlooked. In an instant, the universe aligns.

On the podcast *How I Built This*, host Guy Raz interviews founders and creators who turned an idea into a hugely successful business, many worth over a billion dollars. In most of the interviews, he asks his guest the question, "How much of your success do you attribute to luck versus your own hard work, intelligence, and skill?"

While the answers are mixed, this question seems to evoke interesting perspectives about the role luck plays in success:

> I have this thesis that the world runs on luck, the question is what you do with it. Everyone gets lucky for some amount in their life and the question is, are you alert enough to know you're being lucky or you're becoming lucky? Are you talented enough to take that advantage and run with it and do you have enough grit, do you have enough resilience to stay with it when it gets hard?
>
> KEVIN SYSTROM AND MIKE KRIEGER, creators of Instagram

> I think luck only happens when you are actively moving and searching for what is next. Start moving. Look for the horizon.
>
> JOSÉ ANDRÉS, celebrity chef and restaurateur

Sometimes, miracles happen when luck is involved. But there's more to it. Luck doesn't happen in a vacuum. Turning luck into success requires people who are prepared to recognize a lucky situation and seize it.

In their book *Great by Choice*, Jim Collins and Morten T. Hansen share results of a nine-year study of what they call "10x" companies. These companies started small and eventually beat their industries by a factor of ten. In their *New York Times* essay "What's Luck Got to Do with It?" the authors share a few stories about the role of luck in 10x success. Their thesis is that luck, both good and bad, is an inherent part of success and entrepreneurship. What the 10xers have in common is "Return on Luck," or ROL. The article concludes:

> Getting a high ROL requires throwing yourself at the luck event with ferocious intensity, disrupting your life and not letting up. Bill Gates didn't just get a lucky break and cash in his chips. He kept pushing, driving, working—and sustained that effort for more than two decades. That's not luck—that's return on luck.

In 2007, Sachi and I experienced a luck event that changed our lives and since then, we've been working to get a return on that luck. Sachi had recently joined the company and we were operating as a team for the first time. Common Craft, for better or worse, was now responsible for the income of our family and we were on the lookout for a spark. Sachi and I agreed that whatever direction we took, we had to have a *useful* offering because usefulness can survive good times and bad. We figured that if something is useful and made a positive contribution, the customers would see value and eventually arrive at our doorstep. By contrast, ideas that made quick income the priority felt shortsighted and didn't reflect our values.

In my online community consulting, I noticed a problem that seemed to be pervasive and growing. The executives with whom I worked were smart, informed, and responsible. They were great at their jobs. But in 2005, the business environment was changing quickly because of social media. These execs weren't prepared for the wave of new ideas, tools, and technologies that were about to wash over them, and they didn't have the understanding required to become an evangelist to their peers or employees. I wanted to help them prepare for the future so they could make more informed decisions and innovate through the change.

In looking for resources that might help, I noticed that other experts weren't explaining these ideas clearly. Those who understood social media tools were often technologists who could speak fluently to other technologists, but not to everyday people. They were cursed with knowledge, which means they knew so much that it became hard for them to imagine what it's like *not* to know. Their explanations seemed full of details and exceptions that made understanding the big picture difficult.

I attended a small conference where a tech CEO mentioned RSS as a new technology everyone should use. RSS stands for Really Simple Syndication and makes it easy to subscribe to a website and receive updates when new content is published. When the CEO mentioned RSS as a useful tool, a man in the audience raised his hand and asked a simple question: "What is RSS?"

The CEO responded, "RSS is an XML-based content syndication format" and moved on. The man's hand went down, along with the confidence in the room. I couldn't believe it. The CEO had a golden opportunity to help this person, and many others, understand RSS, which he had just described as useful. And those were the words he chose? After the talk, I huddled with a few attendees and explained RSS to them in a way they could understand. They were thankful, and I felt strongly that this was the problem I could help solve.

At the time, the online video revolution was building serious steam. YouTube launched in 2005 and Google purchased it in 2006. I became convinced that YouTube would kick off a new set of innovations for businesses and individuals. It was a new form of social media that made video a medium for the masses. With Sachi onboard, we had the bandwidth to experiment. We started to consider the potential of making videos that were both educational and useful. We'd use my old blog posts as inspiration for videos that explained RSS and wikis. We thought making a couple of videos to share on YouTube might be a way to solve a problem and maybe earn attention for the company, but we weren't thinking of income at the time.

Within a couple of days after our initial spark, I was in our basement preparing a kind of DIY studio. In a tiny green bedroom with seven-foot ceilings, I hung a whiteboard on a wall and gathered markers and an eraser. I set up a little video camera we had used for travel on a tripod and changed into a button-down shirt. That represented the full extent of my knowledge of video production.

I had never lectured in front of a camera or learned about the basics of video production. There was no special lighting or even a script. But I decided to make the best of it. Alone in the tiny room, I clicked "Record," stepped in front of the camera, and immediately felt like a complete fool. I stuttered, lost my train of thought, scribbled an unintelligible series of arrows and boxes on the whiteboard, and eventually gave up. I can still smell the fumes from those dry-erase markers and the singe of my faltering confidence. It was amateur hour at Common Craft. When I watched the footage, I was deeply discouraged and more than a little embarrassed. It was clear I had miscalculated; making this kind of video would require much more know-how and effort than I expected.

But all was not lost. Within an hour, Sachi said, "What if we laid the whiteboard on the ground, pointed the camera down onto it, and used only our hands, markers, and pieces of paper to explain an idea?" This was it—the lucky moment that changed our lives. We didn't know it at the time, but

Sachi had invented a style of making explainer videos that would become known around the world as Common Craft Style and define our work for years to come. What seemed special about this approach to video was the lack of a talking head with expressions and body language. By using only hands in the frame, along with simple artwork, we could keep the focus on the content and not on the people making it. This style was repeatable, unique, and unquestionably handcrafted. Viewers said it reminded them of looking over someone's shoulder to learn.

We immediately started working on a video to explain RSS, and gathered anything we could find to make this new style work. We pointed bedroom lamps onto the whiteboard on the floor and created a basic outline of points we wanted to cover. For the visuals, on a piece of white paper I drew a messy image of a person on a computer and cut it out. I did the same with boxes that represented "blogs" and "news." Using the paper cut-outs and a marker on the whiteboard, I explained why anyone would care about RSS and spoke directly into the microphone on our basic video camera. Here's a key section of the script, which demonstrates our simple style of explanation:

> This is you, and here are your favorite websites. You log on to your computer, and you're looking for something new. You go out to your favorite blogs. Anything new? Nope. You go out to your favorite news sites. Anything new? Nope.
>
> Every time you look for something new and it's not there, you've wasted valuable time. This is the old way. Now, let's consider the new and fast way, which simply means taking these arrows and turning them the other direction. This means that new things from blogs and your favorite sites come to you instead.

From a video production standpoint, we had no idea what we were doing, and it showed. At the time, it just seemed like a fun and kind of crazy experiment. We were total newbs. Over a few days, we edited the video and took the time to brand it with our names, Common Craft logo, and website. Not knowing how to add text to the screen digitally, we printed pieces of paper with the branding and put it in front of the camera. We called what we were doing "The Common Craft Show" and asked a graphic designer friend to whip up a logo for it.

On April 23rd, 2007, we uploaded the three-minute and forty-four second video to YouTube and called it "RSS in Plain English." "In Plain English" seemed to capture our intent; over time, it became part of the Common Craft brand. I embedded the YouTube video on the Common Craft blog, published the post, and emailed a group of friends. Within minutes, the video was getting comments and views on YouTube and our blog. I clicked refresh over and over, and the number of views climbed and climbed. Comments started to arrive faster than we could read them. It felt like we had released an idea into the world and the world was responding.

I paced the floor, obsessively checking the stats and comments. I took deep breaths and asked Sachi, "Can you believe it?"

Of course she could. Sachi was happy and excited, but as always, in absolute control of her emotions. Meanwhile, I was like a five-year-old kid on Christmas morning, bouncing off the walls. At that moment, our careers and lives were changing at warp speed and we were just starting to feel the pull.

That night, I went to sleep checking the stats, responding to comments, and dreaming of what was to come. The next day the video appeared on the front page of digg.com, the clearinghouse for buzz on the web at the time, and promoted even more sharing. Websites like Technorati tracked links between sites, and Common Craft was adding hundreds of links a day.

Bloggers were a huge part of the video's initial success. They loved RSS because it helped them build an audience. If readers subscribe to a blog's RSS feed, they're more likely to become regular readers because they're notified when new posts appear. The problem was that RSS seemed confusing to their readers and they lacked an efficient way to explain it. When our video came along, bloggers around the world noticed and embedded our video on their websites. Problem solved.

As the initial excitement wore off, we started to ask ourselves: *are we one-hit wonders? Can we do it again?* We decided to make another video called "Wikis in Plain English," and we agreed to learn from the successes and failures of the RSS video. We asked a question that came to be a mantra for us in the process of learning how to make Common Craft videos: *what sucks the most about this?*

While the RSS video was successful, it was a technical abomination. What sucked the most about it, in our judgment, was the audio. The microphone on the camera was low quality and the sound in the tiny basement room made the voice-over sound like it was recorded in a racquetball court. Fixing the sound became our goal for "Wikis in Plain English," which was published about a month later. It was also a viral hit that remains one of our most viewed videos (currently over 2 million views on YouTube alone).

We were in pure DIY mode and simply doing what made sense at the time. We didn't read books or take classes on video production. We stumbled through and solved problems as they came up.

I sometimes consider what would have happened if we had stopped before the first video and learned about video production or education. What if we took the conventional route? Looking back, I'm confident our results would have suffered and we may have missed the window of opportunity.

We were obviously two people making a video in our basement, and that was a feature people loved most. What the videos lacked in professionalism, they made up for in communication. They were the clearest, most effective explanations of social media at the time and the response indicated that a niche was finally being filled.

The videos we published in the spring of 2007 are now known as the first explainer videos of the YouTube era and we became known as professional explainers and originators of a new communication style. The initial videos helped establish a new genre of online videos that made explanation, clarity, and understanding the goal. In the context of business success, this was a relatively small event. A couple of homemade videos went viral. Today, it happens on a daily basis. But for us at the time, it was the spark we needed to start experimenting.

I think luck played a role in jump-starting our story and much of it had to do with timing. I was coming out of school just as the internet was emerging as a resource for businesses. I was lucky to read books like *The Cluetrain Manifesto*, by Rick Levine and colleagues, which inspired me to pay attention to online communities. I was lucky to work for a company that was open to my ideas just as online communities were becoming popular. This experience set me up to be a consultant in an emerging field. Then, YouTube appeared just as Sachi became part of Common Craft, and provided a platform for solving our central problem. We were also lucky to have space in our lives to dive into a video project that didn't appear to have any chance of earning money.

At a higher level, we were both lucky to be born to stable, supportive families and in locations that gave us safety and security; as Warren Buffett said, regarding his own luck, he "won the ovarian lottery." Innumerable people and connections came along and influenced our thinking and direction. And of course, we found each other, which is the biggest luck of all. But it was our determination to get a return on that luck which enabled us to grow a business that could support us for the next decade.

THE TAKE HOMES:

→   If luck shines on you, be prepared to seize it and run with it.

→   Attention is a powerful asset. Experiment with ways to earn attention and be ready to convert it into a business opportunity.

→   Look for opportunities to create something useful and solve a problem. Quick income schemes come and go. Utility endures.

→   If you're sharing something publicly, be sure to brand it. You never know when an event or person will come along and pluck your work out of obscurity.

→   Improvement happens incrementally. Rather than trying to solve all the problems, fix what sucks most and try again.

→   Be yourself, even if it means looking like an amateur for a while. A lack of polish can make your work relatable and unique.

Work for Hire

BY THE END of May 2007, our entire catalog consisted of just two original videos: "RSS in Plain English" and "Wikis in Plain English." My consulting practice started to look small in comparison, and it didn't take long for me to realize that my consulting days were over. Our plans for Common Craft's future became moot as our days filled with a whirlwind of juggling emails, wondering, and worrying.

As exciting as it was to see the videos earn attention, our financial reality was essentially the same as it had been. At the time, YouTube's Partner Program was not available for advertising revenue and there was no way to earn money from video views and comments. We knew there were probably opportunities to come, but it seemed like our initial success had just offered attention, not income. To keep making videos, we needed to find a way to support ourselves. Yes, we were in a unique situation because we had early attention. And yes, that attention meant that we had opportunities.

But what's relevant to every entrepreneur is what we did with that attention.

By June 2007, I added a "Hire Us" link on our website and we started to receive emails from companies who wanted custom videos that explained their products. A conspicuously vague query from a Gmail address seemed particularly enticing, even if we couldn't put our finger on why. Sachi did some reconnaissance, and thanks to the person having been a speaker at a conference, we discovered the company behind the email: Google. Google was contacting us about producing a video. Little home-based Common Craft could work for Google! We danced around the living room before the anxiety set in.

Just two months earlier, I was an independent consultant and Sachi's experience was in managing projects with hospital software and data. We had approximately zero experience in the creative side of business. We had no idea how creative agencies priced their work, planned creative projects, or worked with clients. We didn't have a contract or a reliable way to create a project plan. We wondered, *What have we gotten ourselves into?* We assumed Google was used to working with expensive agencies with refined processes and slick tools.

This all felt eerily familiar. Years before, I felt the same way when I started consulting. I was inexperienced and tried to remedy those anxious feelings by planning everything I could. I over-thought every possibility, and it was counterproductive. This time around, I tried to keep things in perspective and solve problems when they needed to be solved instead of warding off issues that *might* crop up.

Having a plan is useful, and it's important to write down what you need to do. The key, however, is to follow through and get started as quickly as possible. Circumstance is an amazing teacher and will show you what's required to accomplish your goal and keep you focused on the path. Unlike planning, circumstance doesn't allow for exploring possibilities and contingencies. It only cares about the problem that's right in front of you, the one which must be solved before you can move ahead.

When we started working with Google, we didn't spend precious time learning about creative agencies and how they do things, and then comparing those established agencies to our start-up. We didn't look for the perfect project planning software. We didn't document and refine our processes. Instead, we let circumstance lead the way.

Google didn't care that we were not a polished agency. Our contact was happy to work with a small team and appreciated our homespun style. It was refreshing to them that we didn't bother with all the details that come with most creative projects at big companies. Being ourselves was an asset. (Imagine that!) We didn't put on airs or try to be the company we thought Google wanted. We were Common Craft, and we did things the way Common Craft does them.

Google hired us to create a video that would explain a new product called Google Docs. I wrote a script that was based on the idea that documents need homes and that, essentially, online homes were better than local homes on computers. The script established the creative direction of the video, and it sailed right through the approval process. Being our second custom video project, no one was more surprised than us.

Next, we created a storyboard and considered the best way to share it with the team at Google. We looked at the software we had at hand and decided to use PowerPoint (Google Slides was not yet a product). We represented the video with a series of slides that included the script and visuals for each scene. Approved. Then, we shot the video on the whiteboard in the basement of our home using paper cut-outs, markers, and hands, in Common Craft Style.

Just before we finished production, we asked Google if our logo and the words "Video by Common Craft" could appear at the end of the video. To our surprise, they agreed and our brand became forever linked with the video. That video is called "Google Docs in Plain English" and today, it's been viewed over 5 million times on YouTube and represents óne of the first commercial explainer videos.

With this branded video out in the world, we were no longer only a producer of useful videos about social media. We were now a services company that could be hired to make videos about products and services. And for a while, we were the only game in town when it came to explainer videos. We had the first-mover advantage.

After the Google video was published in September 2007, we started to receive leads for custom video projects every day. Dealing with this side of the business was exciting, time-consuming, and stressful. We were working long days producing custom and original videos. Working on responding to new leads, creating agreements for new projects, and having almost daily client meetings seemed overwhelming.

What I remember most from that period was continually saying "no" to interesting projects and knowing we were leaving money on the table. Things were moving so quickly that we didn't have time to take a step back and think strategically. Hiring was an obvious path out of the pressure cooker, but we resisted because we feared that in the tumult, we could make a rash decision that could trap us in a situation where our autonomy would be compromised. We were earning more income than ever, but it came with potential costs to our lifestyle and happiness and it seemed likely that those costs would rise over time.

A couple of video projects during this phase took our visibility to new levels. Dropbox hired us to create a video for their front page. At the time, Dropbox had about a million users and was growing quickly. They saw that growing even faster required a clearer explanation of why anyone should care about their product. That video was the central content on their homepage for over three years and earned over 30 million views as the company grew to serve over 100 million. The video wasn't branded, but by then, Common Craft Style was recognizable to many.

We also created a video to explain Twitter that was like our videos on RSS and wikis. It was an "original" video, meaning that no one paid us to create it. I became a big fan of Twitter and saw that it had an explanation problem that could be solved with a Common Craft video. When the video was almost finished, I wrote to Biz Stone, co-founder of Twitter, to share it with him. He loved it and within weeks, a button appeared on twitter.com that said, "Watch a Video." The video was "Twitter in Plain English" and above it was a link to our website that said, "Thanks to our friends at Common Craft." That video received over 13 million views and helped people see Twitter from a new perspective.

Our relationship with Twitter happened without money changing hands. We made the video because we wanted to explain Twitter, and on a whim, I contacted the company to let them know. We took the initiative, and that email to Biz set up years of free visibility for our brand. My only regret in publishing the Twitter video was not including my Twitter handle at the end. I don't know why the idea never occurred to us, but it could have been incredibly productive in terms of engaging a much bigger audience on Twitter.

One of the videos that people remember most from that era was a satirical video called "Zombies in Plain English," which explained how to survive a zombie attack. It was the first and only comedy video we made and it was an early expression of our independence. We could choose to spend our time on a video about zombies.

As long as demand for custom videos kept flowing, we could earn significant income for a home-based business. Our prices crept up with each project as we looked for the market ceiling. Being unique and in a market we didn't understand, pricing seemed like the best way to manage the demand. It didn't take long to be seen as a premium producer of custom videos that came at a premium price.

But now that we didn't have to worry as much about income, we had other worries. We were becoming restless and burned-out from working long hours. Our lifestyle was suffering and with it, our happiness. As a married couple working from home, the stakes were high when it came to maintaining our personal lives.

Often, the stress and fatigue manifested in small but significant ways. The process of producing the animated scenes of a Common Craft Style video took half a day and came with several frustrations, especially early on. The shop lights we used to light the whiteboard were bright and hot. The camera always needed new batteries and film cassettes. Long stop-motion shots could be ruined by a slight movement of the camera or whiteboard. It was exhausting.

We also had different approaches to work, which came up at every stage of production. In one case, I remember taking what I thought would be a short break before finishing a video shoot. When I walked into the kitchen, Sachi was preparing a hot meal for us both. While I was expecting to grab a quick snack, she saw the potential to have dinner before finishing later in the evening and didn't tell me about the change of plans. In any other situation, this would be a nonevent and I'd be thankful for her thinking ahead. But on this day, in the heat of a long production project, I was unreasonable and frustrated. I said, "What you are *doing*? I thought we were going to finish?" Then we were both frustrated.

The tumult wasn't limited to work hours. Work and home were the same for us and if we didn't find a way to get along while working, everything could fall apart. One of the obvious paths out of that situation was creating an agency, complete with office space and a team of producers. As a service producing custom videos, we could grow. We had the demand to make it work. But we were skeptical. Were we destined to run a services company and make custom videos?

This question set up one of our most important and productive debates. Nearly every indicator in our business pointed to custom videos as the path forward. Being entrepreneurial, we saw the potential to grow and it was enticing. But we didn't want to settle for what appeared to be our destiny. We weren't passionate about running a creative agency and managing producers. Sure, it had growth potential, but instead of building a service company with employees and associated overhead, we wanted to stay small and agile, and be free to experiment. We were intensely interested in the potential to explore what was possible with the attention we had earned, and to get there, we had to reduce drag and avoid traps.

Building our business around custom video work also seemed like a long-term risk. Our video style was popular because it was fresh and unique, and we both saw that as a liability. We compared it to fads that dominate advertising. We didn't want to put all our efforts into our custom work, then see it burn bright and fade away. After all, it was the only style of video we knew how to produce.

Further, we wanted to be educators with full creative control. We created our first videos, like "Wikis in Plain English," to educate and inform. To me, these were the "real" Common Craft videos and they solved a problem for the public. We never set out to make promotional videos or help sell products. Being paid to create Common Craft videos sometimes felt like we were making commercials. I felt like we were a band with hit songs who could be paid to write jingles for corporate products. And our original videos were the true source of our attention. During all the custom video work, we continued to publish original videos every month. Each one was designed not to promote a product, but to explain an idea and be useful. For the first couple of years, publishing original videos was an event. People were excited to see the videos and share them. The success of the Google Docs and Dropbox videos aside, that rarely happened with custom videos.

We felt stuck. Our custom videos were producing income and creating worry. Our original videos were earning attention, but no money. And our lifestyle of constant work felt unsustainable. Then, a small detail in our contract created an opening in our thinking. The light it created became a beacon that guided us for years.

Each custom video project required a contract that stated the scope of work, pricing, schedule, and all the regular legalese. On one occasion, a client's attorney reviewed the contract and wrote:

> I would like the language in the agreement to state that this is a "work for hire" relationship and that [Common Craft] is assigning all rights to the video/deliverable to us. In short, they may be the authors of the video, but it is our video.

At that moment we learned a valuable lesson in owning what you create, and it all came down to those three words:

"work for hire." I think those words are among the most powerful in the creative world. It all comes down to the power of ownership and specifically, ownership of copyright. As we would soon learn, the phrase "work for hire" is a cleaver that cuts through all the details and defines, at a fundamental level, the most basic concept of the contract: who owns what.

For rookies like us at the time, it was easy to overlook this clarification of ownership. It sounds so straightforward on the face of it: a client hires us, we make a video, they own the video and can use it however they want. Easy peasy.

But it's not that simple. Because we created the video, we owned it by default according to copyright law. As the copyright owners, we could do whatever we wanted with the video. Without the words "work for hire" in the contract, we could be hired to make a custom video and then sell it to another company, distribute copies, or use it in our own advertising. The same is true for wedding photographers. Because they take the photos, they own the copyright by default and have the right to control how those photos are used. Intellectual property is a pillar of the creative world. Creators own what they create and it's up to the creator to negotiate ownership or transfer rights when a client is involved. When we sent a contract without including "work for hire," ownership of the video copyright was ambiguous, and defaulted to us. Before spending money on a custom video, the client wanted to be sure that they owned it.

This realization grew in importance over the years. We could make good money creating custom videos, but we'd never *own* anything. Each project meant transferring ownership to the clients. For most creative companies, this is just the cost of doing business. They are not in the ownership business, they are in the services business, and that doesn't rely on owning intellectual property.

This lesson reframed the value of our original videos. The growing library of videos we produced ourselves were not "work for hire" projects. We created and owned the videos outright. We had the right to make copies. We soon realized that we were building a library of intellectual property that we could put to work. The problem was, we didn't know how. We didn't yet see the potential of licensing and using our copyrighted videos as a product.

After long days and constant debate over dinner and dog walks, we decided that we'd keep producing both custom videos for clients and original videos for our library, without hiring. We'd also look for opportunities to capitalize on the original videos we owned.

As this was happening, we kept seeing demand grow for custom explainer videos and we thought it was a shame not to provide supply for the demand. This realization prompted us to consider how we could play a role in matching custom video leads with producers. Our first experiment in getting a return on luck was about to begin.

The emergence of explainer videos attracted attention from brands and video producers who saw an opportunity. More video producers were adopting explainer videos as a specialty and potentially becoming our competitors. Our little niche was becoming more crowded.

Watching this happen, I couldn't help but think of the book *Blue Ocean Strategy* by W. Chan Kim and Renée Mauborgne. They describe a situation that is very familiar to entrepreneurs. The basic idea is that companies have a choice in which markets they compete. They can innovate to compete head-to-head with the competition (a red ocean of low margins and limited growth) or they can innovate with the goal of discovering or developing new markets (a blue ocean where competition is irrelevant). The fundamental idea is that with a blue ocean strategy, you beat the competition without competing against them.

When we saw producers making explainer videos, we saw that we had a choice. We could compete head-to-head in the custom video market where there would likely be a price war, or we could look for a blue ocean. If we chose to compete, we'd be playing the same game as everyone else and as a tiny company, the competition might be able to sink us. But we had a unique market position. We originated the genre and dominated the attention in the market. We could think differently.

Every day, leads for custom videos arrived in our inboxes and every day, we said "no" and those leads found other producers, who were becoming our competition. This seemed like a missed opportunity that could eventually erode our position in the custom video market. So, we set out to find supply for that demand. If people came to us with a need, the thinking went, we might be able to offer a matching service. We could become a marketplace for producers of explainer videos and companies looking to hire them. Instead of competing with producers, we could partner with them by pointing our excess demand in their direction.

In late 2008, the Explainer Network was born.

I carved out some of my time to look for producers who were claiming to produce explainer videos, and evaluated their work. If it was high quality, I would reach out to them with an offer. They could pay a monthly fee and become an Explainer Network member, which entitled them to a branded listing on the Explainer Network page of our website. Then, when people came to Common Craft looking for custom videos, we would point them to the Explainer Network page, where they could contact the producers listed there. It was our own little producer marketplace.

This kind of marketplace business is not at all uncommon. The Explainer Network was similar to online marketplaces like Fiverr and Upwork. These companies offer a place to connect freelancers with customers and earn money by taking a small percentage of the transaction while making the process easier and more efficient, or with an assurance of quality. Another example is Etsy, which connects creators and customers. Offline, farmer's markets and malls are marketplaces that operate similarly.

We'd be operating the Explainer Network on top of our full-time jobs, so we needed it to be lightweight and easy to manage. We asked a question that became a driving force for our business decisions: *what if it works?* If this idea catches on, how does it change Common Craft? If it works, will we need to hire people? If it works, will it ruin other parts of our business? If it works, how will it scale?

We considered a traditional revenue-sharing relationship, wherein we would earn a percentage of any income that came from a custom video project that originated from the Explainer Network. At the time, it seemed like it would be painful to manage. Creating a system for validating what came from the network (or not) seemed like a heavy lift and source of future problems.

In the end, we decided that the most lightweight approach would work best. Producers would pay a flat fee, every month, regardless of the amount of business that came through the Explainer Network. As such, our income from the Explainer Network had a ceiling, but it was reliable and required almost no management. This balance of income versus overhead was becoming a bigger part of our mental calculus.

What started as a few producers eventually grew to a maximum of nine. As long as demand kept flowing to our members, they kept paying the monthly fee. For the first time, we felt like we were making money in our sleep—and that taste of passive income was heady and addictive. It wasn't a business idea destined to become Common Craft's focus, but it was certainly big enough to pursue while the demand lasted.

This kind of cooperation was also good for our brand. Being market leaders, we could create a situation, at a very low cost, that kept us ahead of the competition and at the center of the market. The competition swam in a red ocean, while ours remained blue. And all the while, we were growing the market for explainer videos and making it more visible.

The Explainer Network created a new direction at Common Craft. The income from the Explainer Network was not connected to our time and effort. Unlike custom videos, which were like gas thrown onto a fire, this income was like the coals at the center of the fire. It burned slowly and constantly in the background. It fed flames, and its warmth was subtle and sustaining over long periods.

The Explainer Network's success instilled in us the idea that we have a choice in how we think about competition and what may appear as threats to our work. Rather than trying to protect our market position at all costs, we started to consider ways to evolve as the market changed. This might mean, over time, giving up business models and replacing them with new ideas that match the current environment.

Unlike building a creative agency, this felt like our destiny. We wanted more than anything to build a business that was big enough to survive, agile enough to evolve, and small enough to manage. The evolution was just beginning and with it, we were starting to question our goals and what we were really trying to accomplish.

THE TAKE HOMES:

→   Circumstance is an amazing teacher. Get started quickly and solve problems as they arise so you're not wasting time or worrying unnecessarily.

→   You get what you ask for. If you are hired to create something, look for ways to make your brand part of the experience.

→   If you have solved a problem, share it. Reach out to companies and people who might be interested in your solution and offer your work for free. Sharing your passion can open doors.

→   If you have demand and are unsure of how to price your work, raise your prices with each new project until you find a ceiling.

→   Your intellectual property matters. Be aware of when you're giving it to others and consider how it could help you in the future. Build your IP over time.

→   When considering a new opportunity, ask "what if it works?" This simple question will help you anticipate the long-term effects of a decision.

→   Forming relationships with competitors may be fruitful. Be open to finding ways to work with them to grow the market for your business.

4

Choice as
a Shareholder Value

I N DEBATING HOW to design Common Craft, we had to
consider which version of entrepreneurship we wanted
to pursue. Did we want to grow and have an army of producers pumping out custom videos? Or could we take a risk
and build a business that's more modest and focused on our
values? We didn't have investors or employees. No one knew
about Common Craft's successes or failures, how we used
our time, or our plans. We were the only shareholders. This
realization led to a transformational idea about the future
of Common Craft as a business, and us as entrepreneurs.

By definition, businesses exist to increase shareholder
value. There is probably no more basic distillation of capitalism. Businesses are formed and optimized to enrich the
people who own them. In the global marketplace, it's a given
that shareholder value is measured in currency. If someone
puts $1,000 into a business and gets back $2,000, it was a
good investment.

Like any business owner, we want a return on the time and money we put into the business, and we had to ask: *what is the shareholder value we want?* We, as the owners and only employees, could decide what value mattered most. Once the company became profitable, we could choose how its future success translated to our lives. Instead of valuing constant growth through expanding the team, opening new locations, or betting on an IPO, we could optimize for independence and lifestyle. We could value flexibility or being environmentally friendly. As a two-person business, it was up to us.

Of course, the dynamics of running a business would still apply; this idea just changed its destination. We'd still have to support ourselves, pay our bills, make a profit, and satisfy customers. We'd still work full time. The difference would be our goals and how they influence our decisions in the business. We asked ourselves: *what does it mean to design a business that doesn't make constant growth the goal?*

We agreed that one of our key values is happiness. Being a married couple and working from home, happiness was one of the necessary ingredients of our lives. If our work didn't produce it, or worse, removed it, all parts of our lives could suffer. The problem is that happiness is squishy. Everyone wants to be happy and has their own idea of what that means. Was it really happiness that we were after?

One of the leaders on the subject, Daniel Kahneman, believes that many people confuse happiness with satisfaction. In a podcast interview with Tyler Cowen, he explains that happiness is a fleeting experience. It's an intense feeling that you may remember, but it fades with time. Satisfaction, on the other hand, builds up over time and indicates the overall success of one's life.

Applied to our experience with Common Craft, I got a dose of happiness when we published a new original video or received a check from an Explainer Network member.

It made my day. But the next day, I started over. While satisfaction involved moments of happiness, it related to understanding what we value.

From our perspective, satisfaction comes from living according to one's values. What you value, whether it's money, time, location, community service, sustainability, work, or family, becomes a part of your decision-making. It becomes a metric, provides context, and is one of the central factors in considering the trade-offs inevitable in pursuing a goal. For example, if we decided that the shareholder value we wanted Common Craft to produce was purely income, we might be prepared to make trade-offs and compromise to ensure higher profits. We might choose to work longer hours, work with big-budget clients, or move to a location we enjoyed less if we thought it could lead to more income. Value is the guide.

Or, let's suppose the shareholder value is location. If one of us had an aging parent nearby, for example, we might value location over other factors. Location would receive greater weight in a trade-off. Our income might decrease, but we'd have satisfaction in knowing that we're caring for someone who needs us.

We asked ourselves: *what value leads to our satisfaction?* Once we could support ourselves and our business, which values would we optimize?

Sachi and I considered the lives of fellow entrepreneurs and business leaders. We talked with them about their lives and paid attention to the factors that seemed to represent their challenges. We read articles about burnout, workaholism, and increasing work-related stress. In our estimation, people were generally happy when providing for themselves and their families. But there were simply not enough hours in the day to work, care for family, and pursue fulfilling activities. They seemed to constantly rush from one thing to another, creating a constant state of busyness. Some of them seemed energized by this state of affairs and spoke of their packed schedules with pride. Others saw it differently. They felt they were making a trade-off between money, family, and lifestyle, with a resulting feeling of being trapped. An accumulation of decisions that had made sense at the time led to few exit ramps or opportunities for change. It was the opposite of satisfaction.

In many cases, these people saw the potential for life to be different, but they had to wait. They needed a buyout, an IPO, or for their shares to vest. Then, they could slow down or retire and focus on "what matters." Their suffering lifestyle was the price they had to pay to get to the next phase. They might be happy day to day, but it seemed like they were trying to make the best of a situation that felt out of control.

Sachi and I came to understand that we had the potential to make lifestyle part of our business design, and that it was a value that deserved attention. We imagined a life where we ran a successful business that produced the money we needed, but also allowed us to have choices in how we lived. That sounded satisfying, even if the trade-off meant earning less money. By focusing on improving lifestyle and choice, we had a shot at escaping the trappings of a life that values money over everything else.

As it turns out, there is evidence that trading money for time could be a reasonable bet. There is little question that having more money can reduce tension when a family is under financial stress. However, once a family can take care of the basics, more money doesn't necessarily lead to more happiness. In fact, money-related happiness may have diminishing returns. A study by David Clingingsmith in the Department of Economics at Case Western Reserve University studied the impact of income in measuring a family's "negative emotions." As one would expect, increasing income decreases negative emotions significantly when income is between $20,000 and $80,000. However, between $80,000 and $200,000, the impact of income starts to fall. Income over $200,000 had very little impact on reducing negative emotions. In other words, money produces happiness up to a certain level where needs are met; then, its satisfaction-producing power starts to wane. The message I take from this research is a life spent only focusing on increasing money may not produce a commensurate level of happiness or satisfaction.

Of course, retirement is a factor in this equation. The money you earn over a lifetime could be used to create happiness and satisfaction in the future via a comfortable retirement, and wealth can be passed on as a legacy. Timothy Ferriss called this the "deferred life" in his book *The 4-Hour Workweek*. Instead of spending your income today, you build up a pile of money to spend in the future. The risk is that you defer your happiness until you're too old to enjoy it. While we are consistent retirement savers, this didn't seem like a good bet. We wanted to work toward satisfaction throughout our lives, starting today.

Having wealth over a certain level can also become a burden that creates stress and time constraints. It could be that the satisfaction-producing power of money has a limit, or even a Goldilocks level: not too little, not too much. Ashley V. Whillans and Elizabeth W. Dunn published a study at Harvard that showed a connection between happiness and valuing time over money. They write:

> Although wealth offers the potential for people to spend their time in happier ways, such as by living in a more expensive apartment closer to the office, survey data suggests

that wealthier individuals often spend more of their time engaging in activities that are less enjoyable, such as commuting and shopping...

Controlling for individual and job-related characteristics, such as the number of hours worked each year, ... when respondents' income increased so too did their feelings of time stress.

All the workaholism and burnout we were trying to avoid was connected to the idea of valuing financial wealth as our path to happiness. Sure, we needed Common Craft to support us and provide a resource for our lifestyle and retirement, but the value we decided was most important was flexibility and the freedom to have a choice. If we could design Common Craft to help us earn a living and give us the flexibility to work on what we valued, and from a location we chose, we predicted our business could be the perfect vehicle for a lifetime of satisfaction. We would have a rare type of freedom: the freedom to decide how we use our time.

Now more than ever, I believe that time is the new wealth, and in the future, it will be more valuable than money to many. It will be the element that people strive to control and design into their lives because it's a source of real satisfaction and freedom. Unlike money, time can't be piled up and spent later. Every day it slips through your fingers. Further, time can be acquired by making up your mind. You can decide to have more time and that means consciously designing it into your daily life.

Being flexible and in control of your time comes with trade-offs. Making it a priority may mean making less money and adjusting to a life that doesn't prioritize bling and overt materialism. It may mean reevaluating what is pushing you to strive for more and more expensive things.

Of course, this perspective doesn't mean "doing without," or that working is undesirable, or that not working is the goal. Far from it. It was more a realization that we had a choice, and decided to pursue work opportunities that balanced income and flexibility.

Instead of keeping up with the Joneses and measuring our success and self-worth by our bank account, we could play a new game with different outcomes. With this decision made, we could begin the process of making that design a reality.

THE TAKE HOMES:

→ Small business owners are often the only shareholders. Once the company is profitable, consider what values the company can produce. What shareholder values matter to you?

→ It's easy to assume that the goal of growth is a given in business. Remember that it's not always required and that business success can take many forms. What are you really after? What will you consider success?

→ Happiness and satisfaction matter, and money is not the only way to achieve it. In fact, at a certain point, money comes with diminishing returns. Ask yourself what drives satisfaction in your life and how your business can promote it.

→ Success is often demonstrated through the acquisition of material things like cars, vacation homes, and fancy clothing. This kind of visible success is not required and may not be a path to happiness. Ignore the Joneses and the Kardashians.

→ Time can't be saved up and used later. The only way to have more of it today is to design it into your life. Taking control of a life that's out of balance starts with making deliberate decisions about how you spend your time.

→ Time is the new wealth. Starting today, you can decide to make it grow.

The Business
of Permission

I F YOU THINK about it, a video file, the kind you would upload to YouTube, is not that different from a software
program like PowerPoint. They are both made of 1s and 0s.
They both work on computers and can be transferred
between them. They were both designed and produced by
people with a use case in mind. It's possible that they are
both owned by a person or organization according to copyright law.

But despite having a lot in common, video files and
presentation software live in vastly different worlds. Fundamentally, PowerPoint is a product. It was created by
Microsoft, and the company owns the copyright to the product. They have the exclusive right to make and sell copies of
the tool they created. When you purchase PowerPoint, you
are not buying the product, you are buying permission to
use Microsoft's intellectual property in the form of a license.
This model, software licensing, is much of what made

Bill Gates one of the richest people in the world. Microsoft can make a product and sell it millions of times. Today, that often takes the form of annual subscriptions that come with new features and support.

The same is true with some video files. A movie studio, for example, might pay millions of dollars to produce a movie, and they own the copyright. With this ownership in place, they can treat the video like a product and make deals with companies like Apple and Netflix based on permission to sell or rent their copyrighted works. The studios can make millions of copies of the video file and offer downloads or DVDs. To make it work, there are big, complex systems for managing rights, distribution, marketing, and advertising. Along with directors and producers, teams of managers and lawyers work to ensure that the video file is used legally and at the right price. Like Microsoft, the studios can make a product and sell it a million times, as long as people are willing to buy.

You could say that Common Craft is also a movie studio, albeit on a much smaller scale. We produce short films and we own the copyright of our original titles. Like a film company, we could make these video files once and sell them a million times. But this thought didn't occur to us initially because it wasn't conceivable that a two-person, home-based company could pull it off. We were just two people producing the videos in our basement. Could we market and distribute them too?

As is so often the case, the adult film industry had led the way in terms of developing a model that is small scale and low budget, with wide distribution and profitable producers. We saw what they had accomplished, but it wasn't clear that we could operate in the same way without making very different videos in our basement.

At the time, our business options were limited. We could be hired to make videos, which we were doing. We could make money from advertising, which was just starting in the online video world. Or, we could work through some kind of sponsorship or partnership. The only reliable way for small producers to earn a living was making custom videos in "work for hire" relationships. Online videos like ours were not yet products.

Our thinking changed in 2008 when our best source of innovation started to deliver: we received emails from our fans with a common theme. They asked us how they could use our original videos for their work. They wanted to show "Social Media in Plain English" in classrooms. They wanted to upload "Social Networking in Plain English" to an intranet so employees could learn. They wanted to include our videos in an upcoming presentation. And they wanted to download video files to make it easy.

At first, we didn't know how to handle these requests, but soon our entrepreneurial senses started tingling. These fans were not only asking for the videos themselves, but for permission to use them professionally. They saw them as a valuable resource that helped them do their jobs. These emails were an early signal that we weren't locked into the same path as other producers and creative agencies. They were lighting the path to discovering what was possible for two people to accomplish in a business that had recently decided to make lifestyle a priority.

These messages told us that our original videos had value. They were useful and solving problems for professionals. If this was true, then those people would likely be willing to pay to download the files and use them. Suddenly, our original videos began to look more exciting. They could become a digital product we could make once and sell a million times.

In hindsight it seems obvious, but at the time this revelation took us by surprise. We saw the potential for passive income through licensing.

Initially, we thought it was a long shot that anyone would actually buy and download a video file from us. As YouTube grew in popularity, the perception grew that online videos were free. People knew us from YouTube; therefore, Common Craft videos were free. This misconception was one of the biggest barriers we had in terms of licensing and selling video downloads.

We decided to experiment. Using a service called E-junkie, we could display a "Buy Now" button next to the videos on our website. With this button in place, any visitor could purchase and download a Common Craft video file. Within two hours of the button going live, we received a digital receipt notifying us that a kind soul had purchased a copy of "Wikis in Plain English" for $18.99.

It's difficult for me to describe the feeling of receiving this email because it wasn't only about money or technology or business. It was the feeling that this was real—we could earn money without billable hours or advertising interruptions. In short: we could make money that was disconnected from our time and effort. If it kept up, we could have the flexibility to keep pushing what we thought was possible. Unintentionally, we had created a resource in our original videos that we owned, and that ownership, in the form of copyright, was making a completely new and unexpected business possible. We were in the product business. Starting then, I became addicted to the "Merchant Receipt" emails that arrived when someone made a purchase through our website. These emails had the power to define my day, good or bad, and my connection to them eventually became a problem. Their appearance in my inbox created a rush of endorphins as I saw further proof that we were onto something.

This opportunity set up a situation at Common Craft that dominated our discussions for years and outlined some of the most important differences in how creative organizations stay in business. It was a battle between two business models. On one side was custom videos, which was a service. We had steady demand and could earn a solid living, but we'd own very little intellectual property. If we stopped booking custom video projects, our income would stop along with it. On the other side was licensing, which made our original videos a product that was disconnected from our time and effort. We could make a video once—according to our own schedule and creative direction—and sell it many times. Further, we could produce educational videos that supported the kind of work and lifestyle that we wanted. But demand was still low, and it wasn't a model that could support us at the time.

We could see for the first time that we weren't operating in a world of necessity. We didn't have to work on a custom video project because it was the only way to stay in business. The Explainer Network and video licensing were offering ways to think about our future that were both lightweight and easy to manage. We had an opportunity to ask: *what business do we want to be in?* Unlike when I started Common Craft, when income was the only goal and services were the only option, we saw that we could take a step back and evaluate the options. We could try to predict how a choice made today might impact our business and lives in the future. At the center of this discussion was the simple question I mentioned previously: *what if it works?*

There is often a big difference between the potential of a business idea and the long-term reality of actually running that business. If an idea works and the business is successful, it will consume your waking hours. In the beginning, the rush of success can obscure that reality. But after the excitement wanes and the business is stable, there is a risk that the business won't be sustainable unless you care about the problem your business is working to solve and the people you serve.

Apoorva Mehta, the founder of Instacart, told a story on *How I Built This* that provided a clear picture of this idea. He moved to Silicon Valley with the intention of creating a start-up, and one of his early ideas was a social network for lawyers. He was excited about the idea and even raised around a million dollars to fund it. But something was missing. "What I realized was that when I got home from work, I stopped thinking about work," he said. "I didn't care about lawyers. I didn't care about what they did in their day-to-day lives. It just didn't matter to me."

Mehta could see that if the idea worked (which it did for a year) his life would be wall-to-wall lawyers and if he didn't care about them and their problems, he was on the wrong track. So he stopped. "I had been looking for good 'business ideas' and they were not necessarily business ideas that I cared about," Mehta said. "That's when I realized that the odds of success in a start-up are so low anyway that you must put everything you have in it. And you can't do that for an idea that you just don't care about."

He quit his own start-up, gave the investment money back, and started over.

"What if it works?" became a cornerstone for evaluating our business and our lives. We saw two basic paths: continuing to make custom videos for clients, or focusing nearly everything on licensing our original videos. It was a classic service versus product decision.

To grow the custom videos side of the business, we'd need to find office space, build a production team, and devote our lives to growing and managing the business. If it worked, we could quickly ramp up our income and build a respectable business on a scale we couldn't imagine. It had huge upside potential and less initial risk. We had the demand and attention to make it happen, but we couldn't get past the potential for the business to trap us in a situation where we wouldn't be happy or satisfied over the long term.

Asking "what if it works?" exposed significant risks from our perspective. We never set out to be promoters or advertisers. We were never interested in running a creative agency or managing people. But was it worth it? Would increased income make up for managing a business every day that didn't align with the people we are? Did we want to spend every day thinking about custom video clients? How would we answer these questions in five or ten years?

At the time, I had a personal aversion to making more custom videos, which boiled down to a feeling that I was not in control. I remember waking up, seeing my calendar full of meetings with custom video clients, and feeling dread. Usually, it was not the people who made me feel this way, but our position as producers. I believed our success came from the creative control we exerted in making original videos. Our special sauce was our approach to communication, and we'd proven that it worked. Over and over in the process of making custom videos, that secret sauce was replaced with marketing language and jargon. I'd find myself wincing as I spoke someone else's words into the microphone. It felt like we were selling out.

Don't get me wrong, some custom video projects were truly a joy to work on, and some created lifelong friendships. But many of them were merely transactional. We were a cog in many large marketing machines, and the sound of the gears grinding was not something we longed to hear.

Further, by performing a service, we wouldn't have the bandwidth to build intellectual property that could be put to work in the future. We'd always be throwing cups of gasoline on the fire, only to see it rage for a few minutes before going out and prompting a search for more fuel. Our business would be like mowing lawns. No lawns, no income. Having tasted a bit of passive income, we could see the difference more clearly.

If we licensed our original videos, videos we made from scratch and owned and cared about deeply, we could help thousands of customers on a self-service basis. We could be much more independent and separate our income from our personal time and effort. We could wake up without thinking about daily meetings with clients, deadlines, or employees. If it worked, we could earn a living doing something we love and retain the flexibility to stay in control.

But it wasn't that easy. The income from licensing was just a fraction of the custom video income and we were not sure it would grow. It would potentially take years to build up enough original videos in our library to license our way to success and even then, it may never reach the levels of income we could earn in months by creating custom videos.

To get there, we'd have to accept significant risk and test our ability to stick to a plan of our own making. We'd have to consider phasing out custom videos, our one true income producer, and focus our efforts on the business of permission.

THE TAKE HOMES:

→ Owning the copyright to your work is easy to take for granted. Think of it as an exclusive right to make (and sell) copies of what you create. Register your copyrighted works with the federal government.

→ The people who are interested in your work are a source of innovation and opportunity. Listen to them and ask them what they want or need.

→ Licensing is the business of permission. In essence, it means selling permission to use your intellectual property. When it works, it can create passive income.

→ Pursuing a "business idea" isn't enough. To stay engaged for the long term, it's important for you to care about the business and its customers. Choose wisely.

→ Be prepared to pivot. Just because a business model works doesn't mean it's the only path. Keep your options open and look for models that align with your values.

6

Designing for the Future

COMMON CRAFT, RATHER than simply going with the flow, was becoming a design project. We were fortunate to have the perspective to see two paths, the time to consider where they might lead, and the foresight to predict what reaching either destination could mean to our lifestyle and the health of the company. We set out to design Common Craft with a focus on the long term.

The success or failure of any design comes down to the goals you're trying to achieve. I take inspiration from Frederick Law Olmsted, the designer of Central Park in New York, who often ignored the need for short-term success and took the long view. In a letter to his son Frederick Jr., he wrote, "I have all my life been considering distant effects and always sacrificing immediate success and applause to that of the future. In laying out Central Park we determined to think of no result to be realized in less than 40 years." Olmsted had the vision and commitment to trade early success for a very long-term outcome. While our timeline for Common Craft was much shorter, we knew that we needed to be patient and focus on the long view.

We came to call this idea "planting the garden you're prepared to tend," and that means not only considering what will grow fast or produce the best fruit, but what will be productive and manageable over the long term. When a business is young and moving quickly, it can be difficult to think about the years ahead. Ideas and plans can take root and start to grow before the long-term reality of managing them is clear. And for some entrepreneurs, that's part of the equation. They're ready to do whatever it takes to make the idea work, even if it costs them relationships, life savings, and well-being. It's part of the design and, to them, an acceptable cost. We are not those entrepreneurs and don't aspire to be. We saw an opportunity to test and potentially redefine what work and success meant to us, and decided to plant the kind of garden that was not possible in our parents' generation. We saw that the internet had unleashed new possibilities for entrepreneurship. Businesses like ours no longer had to play by the rules.

For most small or lifestyle businesses, scaling up the business isn't a big priority, as growth may work against their goals and values. Not every barber needs or wants to dominate the market. Product businesses scale more easily than service businesses. Once they get traction, they can earn exponentially more income by rapidly growing their sales with a minimum of expense. That's often the goal of technology start-ups. They scale their way to profits and market domination by using technology and intellectual property to do the heavy lifting. What we saw in Common Craft was the potential to have a hybrid approach. We imagined a situation where we could remain a two-person business but run a company that scales like a technology start-up.

Before getting into the details of the transition to our new way of thinking, I think it's important to look more closely at the nature of businesses like Common Craft and how they intersect with the people who run them. While we were a couple working from home, this dynamic is not that different from co-founders who work together. They also have a personal relationship that is connected to the business partnership; if that personal relationship is compromised, the business could suffer. When partners disagree about fundamental parts of the business, the stage is set for problems.

What Sachi and I shared was our values and our vision of what we were trying to accomplish. This is what makes the idea of "Big Enough" scalable. As long as everyone agrees on values and vision, there is no reason a larger business can't choose a path that optimizes for their unique shareholder value. A ten-person consulting firm could choose to make limited growth, remote work, longer vacations, and Fridays off a priority as long as they agree to accept the risks and costs that go along with those decisions.

This realization laid the foundation for our plans. We had a strong position in the market and a reputation for being experts at explaining technology and the internet. If we could position ourselves just so, Common Craft could become the company we wanted to run.

These ideas, of course, are not what you learn in business school. When Sachi earned her MBA, there were no lessons on making a happy marriage a priority or how a business can contribute to the owner's lifestyle. In thinking about the possibilities and all the assumptions about business, we saw that some of the old rules may no longer apply. To get there, we needed both a plan and a commitment. In late 2008, Sachi and I made a promise to each other that was based on constraints. We both knew it was unconventional and risky. If it worked, it would take years to develop and may never produce enough income to support us. But it could also produce years of income and happy customers, with a minimum of attention. If it worked, we'd have room in our lives for more experiments within the same constraints.

We had to choose. We talked about our tolerance for risk and our true priorities. These discussions, while tedious and sometimes repetitive, helped us decide which path to take.

Eventually it all came to a head one afternoon. Work was done for the day, and I made a cocktail for us both as we relaxed in chairs that faced one another by a window over our backyard. Ambiguity about the future and the constant pressure of competing priorities had to be resolved. It was time to make a decision and start putting a plan into action. The path we chose that day was to focus all our efforts on building Common Craft around our original videos and phase out custom videos. Starting then, we placed a long-term bet that we could make Common Craft a company of our own design. We would be in the product business and earn a living based on our intellectual property.

I shook my head and wondered aloud if we were a little crazy. We were choosing to leave money on the table and bet our future on a business that we had only started to understand. I felt we were making a clean break and part of me loved the adventure of it, even if it was a risk. I was ready. But Sachi insisted that we make the break gradually and phase out custom videos as licensing ramped up. Driving it all was a belief that our business could produce a different kind of shareholder value. The business we imagined sold digital products we created and owned through a system we managed end-to-end. This efficiency and product focus meant that the business could scale with very little overhead or ongoing management. It could be a business that matched the size of the lives we wanted to live. And if it worked and produced passive income, we could have control of our time, be self-directed, and go camping on Tuesdays instead of the weekend. That was the dream.

Once the decision was made and we adjusted to the new reality, we focused on what would be required to put that plan into action. This plan wasn't just about marketing or product development; it included business strategies and lifestyle goals. The constraints we agreed upon, like most constraints in design, were liberating. They narrowed the possibilities and forced us to find creative ways to solve problems. We first saw this power in creating Common Craft videos. To maintain the look and feel associated with our brand, we defined the constraints of our videos to only use a whiteboard, markers, human hands, and pieces of paper. By constraining the materials, we could focus on the content and cut through much of the noise that comes along with creative projects. Similarly, we saw constraints as a way to ensure that the business stayed flexible and manageable. The constraints came down to four related elements:

- Size
- Business models
- Timeframe
- Workplace

The most fundamental constraint was size and a decision never to have employees. We agreed that we would remain a two-person business no matter what opportunities came our way. While this constraint limited our potential for traditional kinds of growth, it ensured we would stay focused on the videos and business without the daily drama and overhead of managing people. This constraint also forced us to be creative in what business opportunities we could pursue. Every idea had to work for two people over the long term.

Staying intentionally small also gave us agility. If needed, our expenses, both personally and in the business, could change to match the conditions. If we went through a phase of very low income, we were prepared for a lifestyle with very low expenses. We could weather almost any storm and that was a key aspect of our new direction with Common Craft. We were prepared to do whatever it took to make it work because it only impacted us.

The second constraint was business models. We decided to focus our energy into licensing our original educational videos and considering them a digital product. We'd also continue to run the Explainer Network because it fit well within our constraints, thanks to its lightweight design. This constraint meant moving away from being a services-based company and attempting to focus on selling products. It also meant saying "no" to more and more custom video projects along with the associated income.

While our intention was to move completely away from custom video services, we knew they would probably remain part of our work. We saw them as a safety net and a trigger we could pull when the right opportunity presented itself or we needed an income boost. When custom videos were a smaller factor, we could be more selective about projects and not get burned-out. For this reason, we prioritized projects that were less focused on marketing promotions and more focused on internal communications. For example, we worked with Intel Corporation over several years to explain their employee benefits programs. This, to me, was an excellent use of our skills.

The third constraint was focused on the timeframe it would take to achieve success. For our plan to work, we needed to give it years to develop and stay committed to our constraints to see it through. After all, our video library was growing monthly, but only contained a few dozen videos. To reach our goal, we needed to think like Fredrick Law Olmsted and plan for the long term.

The fourth constraint related to workplace. Common Craft headquarters was our home and we could not imagine working anywhere else. Any opportunity that took that away would not be considered. This also meant that we needed to make our home the place where we wanted to work and live for the long term.

Together, these constraints represented our path to building a different kind of business. We didn't know if it would work, but we were absolutely convinced that it was worth pursuing. Our small team made a commitment to see it through.

THE TAKE HOMES:

→ Design for the long term. Take time to consider how a decision today might look in five years. If your model takes time, be prepared to weather the storm by reducing expenses.

→ Relationships matter. Whether you're a married couple or business partners, personal relationships can impact the business. Be sure you and your partner share the same vision and values.

→ It's okay to be small. Small businesses can be agile and scrappy. And today, through online opportunities, small businesses can scale.

→ It's not enough to plan a new path. At some point you need to take the plunge. If you're in agreement, set a date and make it happen.

→ Change is easier while working within constraints. Make a list that represents what your business is and, crucially, what it isn't. This list becomes a guide for decision-making by creating rules that must not be broken.

→ Decisions don't have to be binary. Choosing a new path might mean easing into and out of new directions. If you stay focused on the end goal, it can be an evolution.

7

A Platform
of One's Own

WITH OUR PATH set and constraints in place, we now had to execute. We put our heads down and pushed through what we predicted would be a difficult phase for our little company. It's not that we risked going bankrupt or that our customers would switch to the competition. It was about enacting difficult policies that would have negative short-term consequences but would hopefully produce long-term success.

For most who knew Common Craft at the time, we were a producer of explainer videos that could be found for free on YouTube. We'd always shared our original videos on the platform, and it was a major factor in our early success. Our videos on YouTube accrued millions of views over time, and our business could not have become so popular without it.

Most video producers saw the growth and development of YouTube as a positive development. Over time, the company's Partner Program offered options for earning income based on advertising that accompanied videos. Finally, producers had the potential to earn a living from original productions. If their videos were hits, meaning they got millions of views, they could earn income. We watched as video producers in our genre, like Vlogbrothers and CGP Grey, became YouTube stars with vast audiences. The same was true with Khan Academy, who was offering, in the early days, tutorials on solving math problems, among other subjects. These producers, like us, were starting to see that the advertising model was not a good match for their productions.

John Green of Vlogbrothers said in 2015, "I and the most passionate creators on YouTube... we're not in the distraction business. We're in the community business, and number of eyeballs is a terrible metric for my business." Vlogbrothers, along with many other creators, started to adopt a patronage model that meant their viewers and fans could support their work through crowdfunding. They created a service called Subbable in 2013, which was acquired by Patreon in 2015. This model supported their continued use of YouTube but with much less reliance on advertising revenue.

Khan Academy would eventually become a large non-profit organization supported mostly by philanthropic organizations. This funding meant that Khan Academy could continue to grow without advertising support and provide free access to its lessons.

At the heart of these decisions is the reality that producing educational videos requires money and the YouTube model meant that the money came from advertising. When we were considering our options, crowdfunding was not on our radar. Patreon didn't launch until 2013. From our perspective in 2010, YouTube and the potential for advertising income was starting to look like the wrong direction.

We were betting our future on selling downloads of our original videos and this was impossible on YouTube. In fact, continuing to share our original videos on YouTube would likely prevent us from selling videos by offering a free alternative. Were we really prepared to give up the one service that was an essential part of our success?

We approached this decision by thinking about the kind of video producers we wanted to become. One way to explain this is by considering the difference between HBO and network TV. They are both television programming, but have very different models. Which did we want to become? Using YouTube was like broadcasting our videos on network TV. To consumers, our work was free but came with advertising interruptions. Our success would depend not on the objective quality of the work, or its potential to educate or solve a problem, but our ability to attract an audience for advertisers who would pay us for the pleasure. The advertisers were the true customers and they paid the bills based on the eyeballs we could entice. If we chose the YouTube model and it worked, we imagined our livelihood being based not on education or solving problems, but feeding the insatiable advertising beast: always more views and more subscribers. I feared that we'd end up creating disposable entertainment because views mattered more than anything else.

Don't get me wrong. YouTube is full of talented educators with large, engaged audiences. Their videos educate and solve problems. But in the end, that's not what we wanted. Views, comments, and subscribers meant very little to us compared to building the business we thought was possible. I felt that earning a living based on the needs of advertisers was a poor use of our skills.

In using YouTube, we were leery of building our empire on someone else's land. Continuing to use YouTube meant our work would always be subject to YouTube's terms and conditions, YouTube's algorithms, and YouTube's needs as a business. This is known as "platform risk" and it means that by using a single service or platform as the foundation for your business, you're accepting the risk that the platform can change or go out of business. Since Google owned YouTube, we weren't worried about the platform failing, but the idea of our original work being subject to YouTube's terms of service felt like a step in the wrong direction.

In licensing our original videos from our website, we saw the potential to be more like HBO, which comes with a subscription fee. HBO programming is consistently high quality and doesn't have advertising interruptions. The content is curated and oriented around a comparatively small audience of paying customers. HBO doesn't primarily serve the needs of advertisers; instead, it serves the needs of customers who expect better quality than they can get on network TV. It costs money, but is objectively better.

If we chose to be like HBO and it worked, we imagined serving a small group of paying customers who supported our work. Our videos would be oriented around their needs and not the needs of advertisers. We would be able to produce videos that solved specific problems, and it could all happen from our website, a platform we own. We would be under no organization's thumb or ever-evolving terms of service.

At the foundation of this decision was the shareholder value we were trying to produce. We didn't value fame or video views or the attention that comes with serving a YouTube audience. With enough time and effort, we saw the potential to become our own little HBO.

If only it were that easy.

At the time, most of our YouTube viewers didn't know we had a website or that we sold video downloads. To be like

HBO, we had to do everything we could to send traffic to our website instead of YouTube.

For the first few years, we published each original video in two locations: our website and YouTube. When you searched for that title, you were likely to see both on the first page, with YouTube consistently outranking Common Craft in the results. Our goal for future original videos was to take YouTube out of the results and provide only one path to our videos: commoncraft.com.

So, we did the unthinkable. We stopped using YouTube and focused on making commoncraft.com the only home of Common Craft videos. From that point on, we published new videos on our website and only used YouTube for videos that were promotions or titles that we wanted to make available to the public, like our video on Net Neutrality.

With that decision, we took the two most important sources of our early success, custom videos and YouTube, out of the picture. Without them, we'd be starting over and to some degree, that was the point. To accomplish our goals, trade-offs were necessary.

Dropping YouTube also meant losing a free video host. We needed a reliable way to share our videos on our website, so we started working with a company called Wistia that is a paid service. Using Wistia, we could embed our videos on the Common Craft website and make *it* the platform. Wistia handled the backend and gave us the ability to easily share the videos and see statistics that mattered to us as a business, like engagement. It helped that we were fans of Wistia's culture and values, and we remain happy customers.

At the time, our decision felt empowering. This was true independence. We alone were deciding what our company would become. If it worked, our original videos could be our ticket to the work and lifestyle we envisioned. If it didn't, we were prepared to weather the storm.

Between 2009 and 2011, we experimented constantly and learned as much as we could about e-commerce and licensing. At the time, there were precious few small companies that were licensing videos or selling video downloads, outside of the adult film industry anyway.

Educational videos that educators were used to seemed to be stuck in the 1990s. The DVDs were made using traditional (and expensive) video production, and the content was boring and stale. Educators had to work through big distributors to license new films, if they could afford them.

Thankfully, our growing library was attracting more attention and new video titles sent people to our website instead of YouTube. People loved that we were small and scrappy and trying to do something different. Teachers and librarians sometimes said they were rooting for us, and that warmed our hearts.

Custom videos continued to be our safety net. They could help us get through a website development or personal project. What kept me engaged on our path was a graph that represented our future. Starting on the lower left is the income from our licensing business. It starts at zero and slopes up gently to the right over many years. Starting at the upper left is income from our custom video business. This line slopes down to the right over many years. Together, these crossing lines explain the transition of business models. As cash from custom projects fell, the licensing business would be there to pick up the slack.

To make it happen without YouTube and custom video projects, we had to think creatively about what we offered to potential customers on the Common Craft website. Because we owned it, we could do almost anything we could imagine. There was no platform risk and we were fortunate to have a team of talented website contractors ready to help. So we asked: *what if it works?*

For example, we considered the potential to create an online community around Common Craft. It seemed like a great way to engage educators and keep them coming back. But was it lightweight? Or did it create drag? The idea certainly had legs, but if it worked, we might lose flexibility. Having been an online community manager, I knew that managing a community can become, well, a full-time job. So we started to regard Common Craft as a utility website, with its primary function being to serve customers who came to download videos.

Because YouTube represented the mental model of online videos for many, we wanted Common Craft to mimic the features people were used to seeing there. Basically:

- YouTube videos were free to watch.
- YouTube videos could be embedded on other websites.

We also needed to account for the feature that was growing in importance for our licensing business: video file downloads. The vast majority of visitors who came to Common Craft were there to watch our videos and found us through Google searches. These visitors would arrive, click "Play," and watch a three-minute video. This data told Google the visitor found what they were looking for, which helped our rankings and drove even more traffic in our direction.

At the time, search engine optimization (SEO) was a popular goal for businesses. It seemed the internet was full of supposed SEO experts who had tricks that would get your company on the first page of results. In some cases, the tricks were exploiting a hole in the system or a shortcut that fooled Google. While these tactics worked in some cases, they were short-lived because they were hacking a system that was constantly being updated. I always took pride in our performance in Google results because we earned it the old-fashioned way: with quality content. That's really our secret and the true source of the traffic we needed for our plan to work. Our website offered what Google's search algorithm liked to see.

As long as that traffic kept coming, we had an opportunity to sell video downloads to the slice of visitors who were educators and needed "presentation quality" video files for use in the classroom. It was simple enough, but there was a problem. If our videos were available to watch for free, why would anyone buy them? To answer this question, we took inspiration from the world of stock photography, which is also built on licensing.

People who purchase stock photos often use them in a professional setting, like an advertising campaign or a brochure. On stock photography websites, you can browse all the photos, but they include a watermark, like a translucent logo or branding that's visible across the entire image. These images are free to view, but no designer would use them in an advertisement. The professional quality version requires licensing.

We started to think about our original videos like stock photos. We edited the videos on our website to include a watermark that said "FOR EVALUATION ONLY" across the bottom third. The strategy meant we could earn traffic—and in turn, Google rankings—from casual viewers and send a message to professionals saying, "Watch it or send a link to a friend, but if you want to use it for your work, we can help with a license." We knew that teachers were using the "evaluation" videos from our website without paying and we learned to accept it as a cost of doing business. Being a free resource for educators was part of Common Craft's DNA and something that reflected our values.

Up to this point, we were selling video files à la carte, meaning that each video or pack of videos could be purchased individually, without a membership or recurring fees. Once their three-year license was up, we would contact them to renew. The system was working, but we had a difficult time retaining repeat buyers and had to rely almost exclusively on new customers. Managing the renewals created drag and we started to consider if the individual purchase model was the future of Common Craft.

Our strategy started to transform when we considered making our videos embeddable, just like YouTube videos. This meant providing a bit of code that a customer could use to display the video on their website. It seemed simple enough, but there was one caveat. To work, our customers would need to have accounts on commoncraft.com. This way, we could prevent the embedded video from playing when their license expired.

Via our need for embeddable videos, Common Craft accounts were becoming a requirement. We had to ask: *if accounts were required, then what else could we do?* Soon an idea emerged that was based on feedback we received from a teacher. This person said teachers might not be able to afford to buy all the videos individually, but they if they could get the entire library, plus future videos, for an annual fee, it might fit nicely into yearly budgets.

That was the spark we needed and it all came into focus. Common Craft could become a subscription service. Instead of a customer buying a video download and leaving, we would offer annual memberships to Common Craft that would provide always-on access to the video library and all future videos. By having an account, users could display, download, or embed the videos.

If it worked, we could serve a global membership and remain a two-person, home-based business with recurring, passive revenue, much like the Explainer Network, but with more potential. We could grow to serve a huge membership who used our website as a utility, which made it easy to manage. This was scalability, at Common Craft size.

The beauty of this decision-making process was that it was our decision. We were free to choose a path and learn from our own mistakes. Success or failure, Sachi and I were solely responsible. Absolute control gave us an opportunity to take risks that would have been difficult otherwise. There were no employees who could lose their jobs if we failed. There were no investors whose money we could spend on a silly idea. There was no board tracking our progress. There was only us, and that was the essence of our business design.

In August 2011, after months of development, our new website and membership service went live. We were finally in the subscription business and offered a library of thirty-six original videos, starting with an annual fee of $159 for an individual. We sold our first membership within the first few hours. We also offered plans for larger organizations, which was an important part of our income.

Anyone could watch the videos for free with a watermark, but if you wanted to use them professionally, you could become a member and embed them, download them, or display from our website, all without a watermark.

It was a big bet on the future of Common Craft and I was nervous. I knew we had a valuable product in videos, but I worried membership felt like a bigger commitment to customers compared to buying downloadable files à la carte.

I was disappointed more people didn't become members right off the bat. Don't get me wrong, it was working. It helped support us. But I wanted more. I always wanted more. I was, and still am, looking for the exhilaration I felt when we published "RSS in Plain English" and saw it become a hit. The need for success with this new model weighed on me personally. I drove the change and felt daily pressure for it to succeed.

When the membership service went live, the "Merchant Receipt" emails that I had been receiving for years took on even more prominence because they were the biggest indication of the membership service's success or failure. I became addicted to pulling the arm of that slot machine and constantly checked my inbox. Sachi noticed those emails were driving my emotions. When the emails told a positive story, my days were bright and optimistic. When the emails didn't arrive with enough frequency, I felt discouraged and pessimistic about our chances. Rationally, I knew a single day's sales were just a data point and the trend was what mattered. But I am not always rational. The emails announcing new memberships were dictating how I felt about myself, our decisions, and our future. For both of us, this had to change.

At Sachi's insistence, I committed to making a big change: I turned those email notifications off. Sachi insisted that what was happening on a day-to-day basis was her business. She does micro, I do macro. She's the CFO, I'm the creative director. I needed to focus on the future and what we could do to sell more memberships.

She was right. I had become so accustomed to the endorphin rushes that each day without them felt bland and uneventful. It seemed like there was nothing to celebrate. Eventually, I regained a better outlook and took a longer view of our work and direction. It was the right decision.

With Common Craft membership live and functioning, we took a step back to evaluate. I may have been disappointed initially, but we had created a new platform that operated within the constraints we set years before. We were still a two-person, home-based company built on a platform we owned. And now, we had a chance to grow the membership without changing that constraint. Whether we had 100 members, 1,000, or even 10,000, the service was designed to require a minimum of our time and effort while satisfying every customer. And through it all, we were still video producers, publishing about one original video a month and occasionally working with a few hand-picked custom video clients.

While I dreamt of Common Craft membership growing to serve tens of thousands, I soon realized that it didn't need to. Continual growth might get us in *Fast Company*, but it wasn't a requirement. As a two-person business, our needs were relatively modest and it didn't take overwhelming success to make a difference. We were satisfied with a relatively small membership that we could support with excellent service.

One of the most pivotal decisions we made in designing the subscription service was to make it renewal-based. Each year, our members had a choice to renew and our job became to hold on to as many members as possible. It's a golden rule in business that keeping customers is more important (and cost-effective) than acquiring new ones, and our business was no different. After the first year of the new service, we started to see annual renewals and that was incredibly gratifying. We now had two sources of membership income: new business and renewals. That's the beauty of subscription services. A primary way we incentivized renewals was to continue publishing new original videos each month or so. These new videos grew the value of the service over time, at no additional cost to the member. When it came time to renew, they had to consider the future videos they'd miss.

We now managed the entire process of creating and distributing our work. From the first word of the script to final edits of the video, we did all the production work. And importantly, we owned the content and had the right to make and sell copies of our videos. The same was true for each part of the sales, marketing, and distribution process. There were no middlemen or organizations demanding a say in the process or part of the income, aside from video hosting and transaction fees. Little home-based Common Craft was using the power of the web to do what formerly took multiple organizations to accomplish. *We* were the platform.

And our market was truly global. We eventually had members in over fifty countries. It's this combination of complete control and global reach that I think is unique to this period in history. Only in the last twenty years have two people been able to create a digital project from scratch and sell it themselves to a global market. The vast majority of Common Craft members joined without contacting us first and it was magical to see the membership system producing income that was not connected to our time. Our fire now had a foundation of coals that could burn without our constant attention, and renewed itself each year.

While membership helped support us, we were not able to give up custom projects yet. But we had enough flexibility and time to keep exploring and experimenting. It helped, too, to discover how our personal spending was connected to Common Craft. Through our expenditures, we had the potential to make our income—and thus our business—go further.

THE TAKE HOMES:

→ The sources of your initial success may not sustain you. Be prepared to find new ways to reach customers.

→ Be aware of platform risk. If you build your empire on someone else's property, their decisions can impact or even destroy your business.

→ Creating media comes with costs and there are more income sources than ever before. Consider crowdfunding to launch and support your work.

→ Make your website the home of your business. There is no replacement for owning and being in absolute control of such an important resource.

→ Traffic from search is powerful and free. Be skeptical of experts with big promises. What matters more than anything is creating quality content that attracts and engages people.

→ If your day-to-day emotions are being driven by data, consider taking a longer view. Focus less on data points, such as the number of likes, and more on trends.

→ Adjust how you evaluate success. A small business can be successful with a small group of dedicated customers.

→ Holding on to existing customers is easier and more cost effective than acquiring new ones. If subscriptions are working, identify incentives to keep customers renewing.

Live the Monetorium

WHEN SACHI AND I first became a couple, it was obvious that we came from different worlds. Besides the fact that she grew up in Hawaii and I grew up in North Carolina, we had vastly different practices and viewpoints about significant parts of our lives, like money.

With Common Craft transitioning to become a business more focused on independence and lifestyle than income, we had to evaluate the role that money played in our lives. If Common Craft did well, we could loosen our fiscal belts. If it faltered, we could tighten them. Our ability to reduce expenses as a household could essentially maximize our income from Common Craft. This important point changed how we thought about our lifestyle and what we could do to maximize it. Before we get into that story, I'd like to zoom out a little.

It's easy to imagine increasing income leading to an increasing number of options in your life. And it's true: once your needs are met, more money opens new opportunities and choices. You might be able to pay off debts, buy a vacation home, or pay college tuition. In many cases, increased income can be helpful and result in long-term satisfaction.

But there is another side to the equation. I think of it as a personal profit margin. If you make a million dollars and spend $999,500, you have very little margin, but you probably have a trove of nice things. If you make a million dollars and spend $300,000, you have a large margin and likely, fewer nice things.

In the context of these margins, I want you to ask yourself: *which scenario is most likely to increase the amount of choice and freedom in my life?*

This question is not focused on the role of nice things, but on the power of having a choice. When spending tracks with income, lives can quickly fill with things that need care and maintenance. They may produce happiness, but also create drag. It doesn't take long for all the nice things to feel like limitations and commitments. The lifestyle you want may come from income, but it also comes from how you think about spending. Often, conscious spending does the heavy lifting in terms of staying in control and having more flexibility in your life.

Over our many years together, it became clear that we personified the two scenarios above. With a bit of extra income, my natural tendency was to acquire things while Sachi's tendency was to hold onto the income so she'd have more options. She compares this approach to how her parents thought about her performance in high school. They didn't encourage her to achieve high grades and test scores in order to get into an Ivy League school. Their stated goal was to help her have as many options as possible and the freedom to choose which university she wanted to attend. The goal was breadth.

This realization of the differences between us created a small rift in our relationship. Once, early on, we were at a store choosing a gift for a friend and as we checked out, I saw a little toy by the register. It was a wiry red figure with bendable extremities and magnets for feet. Just before the cashier finished, I grabbed the figure and added it to our purchase. When we returned to the car, Sachi looked at me and said, "So, you're the person who buys that crap by the register. I always wondered." I was taken aback. In my mind it was only a couple of dollars and I thought it was something fun. But for her, that purchase went against everything she had learned about money.

Sachi and I met at work and in our first year together, we both received a small year-end bonus. Knowing it was coming, I had planned what I would buy and could not get to the store fast enough. I bought an early iPod. Once again, Sachi shook her head. It just seemed so irresponsible to her. Her bonus went to paying off student loans.

I felt that income was a reward for hard work. If income goes up, you spend it by rewarding yourself in the form of nice dinners, vacations, or a new car. At the time, that seemed like how one lived the good life. I still contributed to my 401k, but my spending happened without much thought or intention.

The difference, of course, comes from our backgrounds.

On her fourteenth birthday, the first day she could legally work, Sachi started a position supervising first graders in afterschool care. From that point on, she always had a job of some kind. She worked part time all through college and full time while going to graduate school. To her, working was a financial game she played. More work equaled more freedom to do what she wanted. From the beginning, each hour of work was an hour that went toward her being an independent adult. We joke that Sachi has been a forty-year-old woman her entire life.

When she and her brother, Mark, were in grade school, saving money became a sibling game. They competed to see who could have the lowest cafeteria bill each month. Instead of always buying lunch at school, Mark sometimes packed dinner leftovers and Sachi took half a sweet potato wrapped in foil. Then, when the monthly lunch bill arrived each month, it was revealed in award show format, with her dad building drama around who won the monthly lunch bill challenge. Sachi has vivid memories of these times and how much joy she derived from the game. It gave her real satisfaction to compete and contribute at the same time. To her, saving money was just a fact of life and a welcome challenge.

Unlike Sachi, my young life was not a challenge. While I didn't grow up wealthy, my parents owned a small business and I had a normal, happy childhood. I rarely knew struggle, financial or otherwise. I was privileged and unaware that life could be different. I was the third child, with my brothers thirteen and fifteen years older than me. By the time I came around, my parents had experienced modest success and according to my brothers, I was spoiled rotten. And there is some truth to that. Both of my parents came from small-town backgrounds. My mom grew up on a farm and never graduated from high school. My dad didn't go to college. But they were both smart, entrepreneurial people with heaps of common sense. Their business success translated into a lifestyle where I rarely had to do without.

I am thankful for them, but I can see now that I grew up not feeling challenged. Our family did not push hard for excellence or achievement. I never felt pressured to make better grades or go to a top-tier university. While I worked for the family business and often had part-time jobs through school, I didn't develop a strong work ethic.

When I was a server at a restaurant during graduate school, I always wanted to be the first one to leave after the rush. I rarely faced situations where I had to put my head down and push through adversity or overcome big challenges. While it was wonderful at the time, I can now see that it prevented me from developing a sense of resilience. As I grew older, I started to push myself a bit more and make decisions that tested what I could do if I tried a little harder. It started by going to graduate school, moving to Seattle without a job, and crafting a completely new life from scratch. Each time I tested myself, I found new satisfaction borne of a bit of strife, sacrifice, and even pain.

Soon after arriving in Seattle, I met Sachi and saw someone who had a different setting when it came to resilience and work ethic and it took me by surprise. When it came time to do a big job like moving or painting a house, I would look for the easiest, quickest way to do it. Maybe we could hire someone or do just enough to suffice. Sachi wouldn't have it. She insisted on doing it all ourselves and spending as little money as possible. All we had to do was apply ourselves and push through, even if it was difficult, painful, or boring. To my surprise, I felt enormous satisfaction from working hard and knowing we spent so little money.

It's within this context that Sachi and I developed a way to manage our spending. Prior to Common Craft, we were young professionals who had a bit of financial freedom. But we also had big goals like owning a home and traveling. Sachi, of course, was good at saving money and managed our finances. I went along with saving money, but I didn't like having to sacrifice. This started to change when we realized we could adopt a lifestyle change designed to force us to be more budget conscious when we needed to save for a big goal. We call this change in lifestyle and perspective "the monetorium," which is a term invented by our friends Sharon Eiler and Ryan Turner.

The monetorium is, at heart, a moratorium on spending money. This, of course, doesn't sound exciting or interesting, unless you're Sachi. Budgets or limitations rarely are. But there's much more to the monetorium than meets the eye, and today I count it as one of the best longer-term life hacks we've discovered.

While the overall goal is to save money, the monetorium represents so much more. It's a change in attitude and a way to work for a reward we both want. It's a way to orient our lives around achievement through small sacrifices, and to feel like we've earned our lifestyle. And importantly, it's a game we play together that gives us more choices. The monetorium is a responsible and resourceful way to achieve the life we want.

The monetorium works like this. We set a personal goal, like a trip or a home improvement project. The goal needs to be something we both want but can't easily afford. In 2015, we had a goal of moving to Charleston, South Carolina, to live and work for three months. In the year before leaving on that adventure, we "lived the monetorium."

There are three basic elements to the monetorium and they manifest in a million ways for us. The basic elements include:

- Doing without
- Maintaining what you have
- Reducing waste

Anyone who lived through the Great Depression or has lived through a war (or even the Great Recession of 2008–9) would know these elements. For many, they are a requirement and if given the choice, many would prefer not to live with these kinds of constraints. To have a choice is a privilege and that's my point. These elements transcend socioeconomics and represent a responsible and practical way for anyone to live.

In practice, the monetorium is a lifestyle that we adopt with intention. We agree that it starts on a specific date and ends when our goal is accomplished. Starting then, we both commit to taking a second look at our habits and daily routines and identifying how they could be removed or modified to save money.

For example, we cook and entertain at home—no big expensive dinners out. In fact, almost no meals out. Sachi builds meals on sale items at the market and we both work to make cooking at home a source of fun and experimentation. We travel locally and camp when we can. We don't buy new gadgets or clothes unless they're required. I drastically limit small luxuries like espresso drinks, rented movies, and subscription services.

We focus on maintaining what we have so we can reduce replacement costs. When clothes start to show wear, Sachi sews up holes and replaces buttons. We keep the recommended amount of air in our car tires. We keep our computers updated and backed up. We learn how to extend the life of different rechargeable batteries. Again, the intent is what matters. Your mileage may vary.

The monetorium also extends to reducing waste. This focus on squeezing value out of everything becomes a game that's not about the dollar savings, but the satisfaction of living more practically. For example, Sachi often bakes bread so we don't need to buy it (and it tastes better). Unlike the store-bought kind, home-baked bread starts to go stale after a few days. Rather than throw older bread away, we cut it into pieces and bake them to make croutons or soak them in a delicious egg bake. These are small things we celebrate. We baked our own bread and wasted none of it. How cool is that? Now, making croutons obviously isn't going to help us pay for a vacation, but it feels incredibly satisfying in the context of the game. There's achievement in both small and big wins. It teaches me to maximize everything in our lives and try to waste nothing. Isn't that how it should be?

The monetorium is a self-imposed mode of living that's lighter, cheaper, and more home-based. It's a time to be conscious of where we spend our money, how we maintain our belongings, and what we waste. And it works, in part, because it's temporary. It has an end date. We can do almost anything for a year. We minimize in order to maximize.

The first time we lived the monetorium was in 2005. We needed to save up for a big trip in 2006 and at first, I was reticent. I was not used to doing without and the monetorium seemed like a bummer. Every time I wanted something and couldn't have it, it felt like a loss to me. But I went along with it and imagined every dollar we saved going toward a nice vacation dinner.

The next time was in 2009 when we needed to save money for a house renovation. By this time, Common Craft was doing well and I questioned if we needed the monetorium. This time around, I started to see it differently. After the first couple of months I got used to eating every meal at home and generally doing without. It became a lifestyle and it didn't bother me. I knew that a return to our normal spending was just around the corner.

Since then, the monetorium has become a familiar part of how we operate. We believe that happiness lives in anticipation. By living the monetorium, we can look forward to achieving the goal and find everyday joy in the game of getting there. It's not unlike planning for a vacation. The happiness derived from planning and preparation may feel even better than sand between your toes.

In the context of Common Craft, the monetorium provided a way for our income to go further as flexibility became our priority. We adopted a strategy that accepted less income in the short term. That meant we had to adjust our personal lives as well. If we insisted on expensive travel, designer clothes, and high-end dinners, we might never reach our goals. However, by living the monetorium, we could choose to simplify our lives and reduce our expenses so that we were more agile. We could get through almost any challenge because our needs were so limited.

Over many years, Sachi has taught me to have a better work ethic and to demand more from myself. She showed me that there is pride in a bit of pain and that hard work is more mental than anything else. You just have to make up your mind. I've come to see this as an important part of my personal evolution. I want to become stronger, more resilient, and as self-sufficient as possible, even if increased income means I don't have to.

Recently, I stumbled upon a movie that captured this feeling. *Lawrence of Arabia* hit theaters in 1962 and is based on the life of a British soldier in wwi named T.E. Lawrence who was active in the Arabian Peninsula. Lawrence was portrayed as an almost superhuman man who, like the Bedouin, could survive in the desert with minimal water. He endured myriad challenges, all while keeping his cool.

One scene in particular stuck with me. Lawrence is talking with a couple of fellow soldiers, one of whom has an unlit cigarette. Lawrence pulls out a match and lights the cigarette. With the two soldiers watching, he then puts his fingers on the match and slowly snuffs out the flame without a flinch. One of the soldiers, named Potter, is mystified and tries the same trick, exclaiming as his fingers touch the flame, "Ooooh! It damn well hurts!" Lawrence's reply is "Certainly it hurts." Potter looks askance at Lawrence and enquires, "Well, what's the trick then?" Lawrence says, "The trick, William Potter, is not minding that it hurts."

Those words have become a kind of mantra for us. *The trick is not minding that it hurts.*

Now, admittedly, the struggle and pain I'm referencing in the context of Sachi and me is symbolic. We are fortunate not to experience real pain or suffering. I recognize that. But I also think too many privileged people lose sight of how it feels to be challenged, to struggle, and to feel a bit of pain.

This is especially true when income rises. Suddenly, money becomes a means for banishing any kind of pain or strife. You can hire a cleaner, mover, or house painter. Checking the car tires gets your hands dirty. This version of the good life means that you don't have to worry about the details. They are someone else's problem and you've earned the right to push those problems out of your life. Besides, you're busy.

In the beginning, the monetorium was a means to an end, but I came to see it as a training exercise. Each time, I grew more and more accustomed to doing without and living more practically. Each time, I grew in resilience and self-sufficiency. I began to wonder, *what if the lifestyle that works best for us is one that* always *values self-sufficiency, saving money, and maintaining what we have?* Isn't that a smart way to live? What if living the monetorium *is* the good life?

Recently, we seem to be transitioning to full-time monetorium mode and deriving real satisfaction from it. I first noticed the difference when we decided to go to a local pub and get a cheap beer and a burger. Prior to this moment, I had not eaten out in about two weeks and I could not wait for that burger. From the moment that burger hit the table, I wanted it to last longer.

That night, I realized that my reward system had been rewired and that I could be happy with a lifestyle that wasn't continually connected to fluctuations in income. Even if I could afford to eat pub burgers or a prix fixe menu with wine pairings every night, it didn't matter. Our perspective had changed, and we came to see value in more simple pleasures. It felt like a relief because my happiness about that burger wasn't connected to income; it was about choices I had made in how to live.

In his book, *I Will Teach You to Be Rich*, Ramit Sethi explains the idea of conscious spending, which is being aware of how you spend money and spending with intent. The key, according to Sethi, is to be sure that your spending is aligned with your goals and values. Spending is a choice that many people take for granted. They lose touch of where their money goes and the degree to which it connects to what they truly value. By being conscious of spending and working to ensure that the money you spend is going toward things that matter, you can get more out of your money.

Some people go through life believing there is some magical level of income and spending that will finally make them happy. The new car was nice, but now it's just sitting in the garage. Maybe a Rolex would do it, or a country club membership? Spending becomes connected to income and the idea that it's possible to spend your way to happiness. This is often referred to as the hedonic treadmill. When your happiness is derived from spending, you have to keep spending to stay happy.

There are obvious risks to living this way. First, as I discussed earlier, money starts to lose its happiness-producing power once your needs are met. Second, unchecked spending comes with consequences that may not be obvious. When times are good, financial obligations can seem like no-brainers. Of course you can afford another car payment. That vacation home is worth it. The problem is that your financial obligations don't care about your income. If income drops, you still owe on the vacation home mortgage each month. Further, every additional asset you acquire might create some pleasure, but it also creates drag in the form of obligations to manage and maintain the asset. This reality may not be apparent until you look around one day and see that you're spending more time maintaining what you have than actually enjoying it. Living in Seattle, I see marinas full of luxury sailboats sitting idle.

In chapter 4, I discussed the unique quality of time and made the point that having more of it is a matter of making up your mind. You can choose to have more time by designing it into your life. It is within your control. The same is true with spending. While you may not have control of things like health and income, you can choose to control your spending. You can make up your mind to spend less and if you do, your income will go further.

You probably can't buy your way to happiness and satisfaction, and in attempting to do so, you risk increased unhappiness in the form of debt and obligations. In fact, there is growing evidence that we are not able to influence our own happiness as much as we think. Most people are born with a set point of happiness that comes down to our biochemistry. In his book *Sapiens*, Yuval Noah Harari says that many scholars see our set point of happiness like an air conditioner that's set at a specific temperature. It may go up or down when the weather changes, but it will eventually revert to the set point. Whether it's winning the lottery or becoming an amputee, happiness often returns to what the person experienced prior to the event.

But it's probably not that absolute. Sonja Lyubomirsky, Kennon Sheldon, and David Schkade set out to find the source of "Chronic Happiness" and proposed a three-part model in their paper "Pursuing Happiness: The Architecture of Sustainable Change":

- About 50 percent of your happiness is biological.

- About 10 percent is based on events and circumstances.

- About 40 percent is based on intentional activity, what you choose to do.

This of course leads to the question: what activities can help? If half my happiness is already set and I have control of 40 percent, what can I do? To answer this question, we can look to the work of Martin E.P. Seligman, a positive psychologist and leader in the study of happiness. He has found that happiness has three dimensions that can be cultivated:

- The pleasant life: a life that successfully pursues the positive emotions about the present, past, and future.

- The good life: using your signature strengths to obtain abundant gratification (through activities we like doing) in the main realms of your life.

- The meaningful life: using your signature strengths and virtues in the service of something much larger than you are.

I think of these dimensions like a ladder that one climbs in an effort to increase the 40 percent of happiness that is within our control. The key, in my mind, is realizing that the highest rung is based on leading a meaningful life by using your strengths in service to others.

Phew. I've just thrown a lot of information and research in your lap, so let's see if we can sum it up.

Money and income are how we often measure success, but they can also create problems. If we start to associate spending with happiness, we can get in a cycle where we must spend more and more just to stay happy. To get out of this cycle, we can be more conscious of our spending and ensure that spending supports our goals and values.

We can also understand that a large part of our happiness may be beyond our control. We may be born with a set point of happiness that isn't likely to change. We are who we are. However, there are things we can do that may promote or develop happiness, which includes building on our strengths and using those strengths in the service of something bigger than ourselves.

We never set out to use the monetorium to find happiness, but in the context of the research, it's hard not to see it as a method for moving in that direction. Having made a commitment to focus on being in greater control of our time in the future, the monetorium gave us even more flexibility. It forced us to be conscious of our spending and adapt to a life where happiness comes from something other than higher income.

THE TAKE HOMES:

→ Attaining the lifestyle you want isn't simply a matter of more income. It can also relate to how you spend that income. A penny saved truly is a penny earned.

→ Once your needs are met, consider the role more income plays in your life. How can you use it to increase your autonomy, independence, and agility?

→ You probably can't spend your way to happiness, but spending can quickly fill your life with commitments and assets that create drag.

→ *The trick is not minding that it hurts.* There is satisfaction to be found in sacrifice and hard work. Banishing these things from your life may seem like a reward; instead, consider them a way to become more resilient.

→ Use the monetorium to achieve a goal through small sacrifices. Challenge yourself to change your habits and live more practically by maintaining your belongings and reducing waste.

→ Question what you consider to be "the good life." By experimenting with new lifestyle approaches, you may be able to rewire your values and find happiness in simpler things.

→ About half of your happiness is biological and can't be changed. About 40 percent is based on your choices and decisions. You may be able to increase your happiness by using your strengths to help others.

Turning Copycats into Customers

HAVING THE COMMON CRAFT membership service in place felt like we had rounded a corner. We spent nearly a year and invested tens of thousands of dollars to get it up and running. If it worked, it could scale to support us 100 percent. The constraints we put in place, like not having employees and focusing on flexibility, were our guide to thinking through what was possible.

It's easy to assume that being in this position meant we could relax. Common Craft's income was steady and mostly disconnected from our time and effort. Further, we had low expenses that made every dollar go further. But focusing on lifestyle doesn't have to mean sacrificing ambition. If anything, this new version of Common Craft meant we had the option to be even more ambitious. We felt we were just getting started because now we could look for new ways to earn a living within the constraints we had set years before. But in the background, we were thinking a lot about one of the realities of increased exposure: the risk of others "stealing" our work.

In the early days, we took an unconventional approach to competition. As video producers adopted explainer videos, we created the Explainer Network, which helped them find business through listings on the Common Craft website. This service was successful for years and helped us see that business doesn't have to be a zero-sum game and competitors don't have to be enemies. In some cases, cooperation can be fruitful and create new opportunities.

Since we published the first video in 2007, there have always been people who copied our style and our fans were the first to point them out. We consistently received emails from people with links to what they saw as obvious copycats. In most cases, these were not competitors, but people who were inspired by our work and experimenting. For the most part, we loved the idea of people adopting the goal of explanation and working to become better explainers, in video form or otherwise. I have always said that a small increase in the explanation skills of the general population would go a very long way. If we could play a small part in that change, it would be a win. Over time, our reputation as explainers started to look more like a business opportunity and one that we thought could contribute something positive. In fact, we were becoming more open to working with the copycats our fans saw as threats.

In his book *Show Your Work!*, Austin Kleon writes, "Teaching people doesn't subtract value from what you do, it actually adds to it. When you teach someone how to do your work, you are, in effect, generating more interest in your work. People feel closer to your work because you're letting them in on what you know." We wanted to help others become better explainers.

An editor at John Wiley & Sons, a large book publisher, wrote to me in 2011. She had long been a fan of Common Craft videos and was curious if I'd ever considered writing a book about helping people become better explainers. We set up a call, and soon the publisher was interested in making an offer. The prospect of writing a book meant we had to think differently about sharing what we considered our secret sauce: our expertise in explanation. It seemed like a risk to me because our process of explaining ideas felt like our property and something we should protect. It seemed like we could be creating future problems by sharing what made us unique. Were we ready to teach it? Were we ready to create our own competition?

We viewed this opportunity like others we'd faced. Sachi had no reservations about sharing our knowledge and her confidence helped get me over the hump. Yes, there were some risks. Yes, it would take time away from making videos. But we designed Common Craft to be able to take advantage of an opportunity like this.

Making this decision highlighted how we had grown to understand more about each other. Over the years, we had made plenty of decisions, but relationships always evolve and need constant tending. In this case, I needed to change. Usually, in thinking through new directions, I am the dreamer and Sachi is the realist. This contrast is an essential part of how our relationship and partnership works. I learned that Sachi isn't cynical or only concerned with risks; she's analytical and rational. She learned that my optimism and idealism are not reckless; they're a source of ideas and new approaches. Instead of taking offense or feeling obstructed, I learned to recognize that Sachi's input was not only necessary and productive, but a strength that we could put to work for the company. Our difference made us more rigorous businesspeople.

Getting to a point where we could talk about this difference wasn't easy. For too long, I was dismissive or convinced about the beauty of my ideas over hers. Though I didn't realize it at the time, I had a habit of discounting Sachi's input or seeing it through the lens of my own ideas and how it might challenge them.

We don't really fight in the way that many couples do, but there are times when emotions boil over and we need time to recover. More than once, Sachi has said, as we debriefed, "We can talk about everything in our lives and I'm good. We can disagree, we can debate, and I'm happy to be brutally honest. But one thing I can't deal with is being dismissed."

Hearing these words, I started paying more attention to our interactions. I started noticing where my mind would go when Sachi would make a point. What I saw was a subconscious tendency to question or discount or dismiss. In the moment, I might think she's being biased in some way or that she's only seeing part of the big picture. I would listen, take in her points and discuss them, but in the back of my mind, I reserved a spot for undercutting them or not fully buying in. Watching this happen disturbed me, but seeing it in action caused me to change. From that point forward, when we brainstormed book titles, or what to do about a Common Craft project, I worked to take Sachi's input at face value and accept it more fully. This didn't mean I had to agree or that her words were written in stone. It was more like creating a situation where her input had a chance to be accepted. I had to work on that voice in the back of my mind that wanted to say "yeah, but…" or "well, maybe…" It helps, of course, that Sachi's input is always thoughtful and incisive. I ignore it at my own peril.

In the case of deciding about the book, it didn't take long for us to come to an agreement. The business allowed us the time to work on it. I developed a proposal and a sample chapter, and it sailed right through the approval process. I felt fortunate that Wiley had bought into the idea. Our brand and reputation preceded us, and our independence created the space for the book to happen.

A driving force behind the book was to establish ourselves as not just video producers, but the leaders of the explainer movement. There were no business-focused books on explanation at the time, which meant, if it worked, we could find a blue ocean. The book would hopefully create more visibility and buzz that we could turn into memberships.

Like so many things, I dove into the book-writing process headfirst and figured it out along the way. Working with a publisher meant working within their processes, expectations, and deadlines. This structure was important and useful, but not always clear and easy to navigate.

I wrote most of the book over a month on Orcas Island in Washington State, which is in the Salish Sea between Seattle and Vancouver, British Columbia. We rented an old house in the off-season that provided a perfect place for a writing retreat.

I don't know if it was the location or our own motivation, but that retreat was one of the most productive periods we've had. Aside from supporting Common Craft members, the book was our only focus—morning, noon, and night—and we fell into a kind of flow that allowed us to shut everything else out. I wrote the words but Sachi reviewed everything, from big ideas to copy edits.

Along with writing the chapters, we started to consider how the book might be an asset for Common Craft. Usually, a book has a way of increasing the author's visibility. If that author is an entrepreneur, the same is true for their company. Because books are not known for their ability to produce much income directly from sales, it helps if the book creates a ripple effect. The pressing question for us was how we could turn book readers into Common Craft members.

The audience I hoped to reach was businesspeople who saw the potential to become better explainers in boardrooms, meetings, and classrooms. I wanted people to see that explanation was a skill they could learn, develop, and apply as a competitive advantage in any medium. The problem was there wasn't a compelling reason for my target readers to care about Common Craft videos. They didn't need videos for educating in classrooms; if anything, they needed ways to create their own.

At the time, we had been producing Common Craft videos for about four years. For each video, I created the artwork. It started completely analog, with each image hand drawn and cut out of a sheet of paper. Then I began to use a drawing tablet to create digital images. This was an important innovation, because it made our artwork reusable and more standard. We didn't need more than a couple of images of computers, for example. We started to collect the digital images with each video and our library grew to over 1,000 images.

Having this library on hand did a few things for us. First, it made the production process more efficient. We could add a digital drawing from the library to a storyboard, print the images, cut them out, and they were ready for the video. The library also helped to define Common Craft Style, which informed future artwork. We started to create images we thought would be most useful across videos.

But the real value of the images wasn't obvious until fans started to ask about downloading them. They liked our visual style and saw opportunities to use them in videos, presentations, documents, and more. They liked that they were all the same look and feel, and were flexible due to their limited detail. Once again, we had to think through the risks of sharing what we considered our brand and intellectual property. If it worked, we would be encouraging copycats and creating confusion regarding our work versus someone using our images.

Up to this point, we had developed a hands-off approach to copycats, in part, because there was only so much we could do. If we wanted to spend a lot of money, there was some possibility of legally protecting our look and feel. But that comes with the responsibility to police it. Were we, a two-person company, going to start sending cease and desist letters to people who were inspired by our work? Most of them were just practicing a fun new video project. Being so hard-core didn't fit with our culture and we didn't want to spend money on legal fees to do it if the stakes weren't high. We didn't want to see large ad agencies copy our style without attribution (which eventually happened) but that goes with the territory.

Instead of trying to protect and police our style, we took an approach that fit with our values and constraints. We decided that we'd look for ways to *help* people copy us and spend time educating them about appropriate use. Instead of fighting the current, we'd go with the flow and cooperate rather than compete. Being a small and agile company, we didn't have the drag that prevents larger companies from evolving quickly as conditions change. Sure, we were taking a risk, but in doing so, hopefully opening new doors.

This approach to copycats and managing our look and feel took on new relevance when the opportunity to write a book appeared. Suddenly, it was obvious. Our visuals, which we branded "cut-outs," could be attractive to book readers because they made it easier to produce videos like the ones described in the book. Someone could read the book, go to our website, and download cut-outs for their own projects.

This was the opportunity we were hoping to find: a valid reason for readers to become members of Common Craft.

And the beauty of it all was that the cut-outs were a byprod-
uct. They were created as part of our video production
process. With each new video we produced, the library of
cut-outs grew. And with the membership service in place, we
had a scalable platform for selling access to download them.

For our plan to work, we had to develop a completely new
library and membership plan, and launch it before the books
hit the shelves. It required very long hours, but with the help
of our contractors, we made it happen.

In the fall of 2012, *The Art of Explanation: Making Your
Ideas, Products, and Services Easy to Understand* was published. The book included a page in the back that promoted
the idea of downloading and using our cut-outs in creative
projects. As the book received more attention, we started
to see traffic and licensing grow. The book was helping our
business, and my worries started to fade. Sachi was right. On
book pages where we discussed specific videos, we added QR
codes that linked readers directly to the videos on our website. From there, they could also discover our cut-outs, which
were starting to contribute to the bottom line. We marveled
at how the book and cut-outs were such a good fit for what
we thought was possible for Common Craft. We could stay
small and sell something that we created and owned.

Perhaps the biggest outcome of the book was something
I accepted only hesitantly at first: public speaking. I began
receiving consistent invitations to speak at corporate events
and conferences. It was stressful and nerve-racking in the
first year, but once I had multiple events behind me and
a more refined talk, I felt more at ease. It helped that the
speaking fees were a contributor to our bottom line and fit
with the Common Craft way.

Once my perspective shifted from "how am I going to get
through this?" to "how good can I make this?" my outlook
seemed to get better. Confidence is key and that comes from

experience. The only way to get over the fear is to stand in front of people and do the work. *The trick is not minding the pain.*

Our strategy of engaging copycats took another turn in 2015 when we saw buzz building around the idea of online courses. Sites like Udemy, Coursera, and Lynda were growing in popularity and people like us, who had expertise in a specific domain, were jumping into the fray. Along with this trend, Common Craft customers and fans were asking for specific information about our video production process.

In the members-only section of the Common Craft website, we give members an opportunity to suggest and vote on video titles they want us to produce. Along with all the strange suggestions like "How to Play Bridge" and "Football for the Football Widow," a genre of suggestions emerged that caught our attention. These suggestions were all some form of "How to Make an Explainer Video" and "Storyboarding for Explainer Videos."

At first, the suggestions seemed a bit out of place. The Common Craft video library covers a handful of subjects like technology, internet safety, and financial basics. Videos about making videos didn't seem to have a home in this context. Plus, the nuts and bolts of the production process felt like the family jewels, the one process we needed to protect. That perception started to change once we wrote a book on explanation and added cut-outs to our membership. We were already pretty far down the road of sharing everything we could.

Over time, those video suggestions bubbled to the top of the list and it was clear that we faced a familiar choice. People were seeing an opportunity to not just copy our style, but to learn about the production process from us directly. We asked ourselves a now-familiar question: *do we approach this as an opportunity or as a threat?* It was clear that this desire among our members and fans represented a new opportunity and we got to work in creating online courses.

I could finally use a domain we purchased in 2012—explaineracademy.com. Explainer Academy's online courses seemed like a perfect extension for the Common Craft brand. Our original videos continued to bring traffic to our website and inspire people to make their own videos. We offered cutouts that could be used in videos, and a book that focused on explanation skills. We were both excited about the potential and, admittedly, I was a little leery of the commitment. We'd have to build, market, and sell two self-paced online courses under a completely new brand. Building the Explainer Academy website and courses would take many months—the equivalent of an additional full-time job. I would take on the brunt of the production work, which meant putting other projects on hold. We had the choice to do this because we were in complete control.

With this decision, we threw out any concerns we had about giving up our look and feel. We were clearly saying we wanted educators to copy our style. While I still felt this could be a risky move, our overall feeling was liberation. We would finally provide the service so many of our fans and customers had been requesting. We were basing our future business on the belief that the enduring value of original Common Craft videos was not the format, but the explanations themselves and, in particular, our writing. We were betting we could continue to license our original work and teach others to create their own.

In August of 2015, the Explainer Academy launched with two courses using the Teachable platform: the Explanation Master Course, which focused on explanations in any situation, and the How to Make DIY Animated Videos course. Both were full of short videos, downloadable documents, and more. We sold a few dozen enrollments within the first couple of weeks. I wanted to believe that the trend would continue and those courses would create a steady stream of traffic that could produce easy income.

But it didn't happen that way. After the launch, traffic died down—and with it, enrollments. Left alone, it seemed the Explainer Academy website would eventually fade into obscurity. Organic traffic doesn't just appear and stick around, it must be built over time and that's difficult for a new brand. We probably should have built the courses onto the Common Craft website, which does have organic traffic. Lesson learned. Over time, we developed more of an audience for the courses and used the Common Craft website to promote it. The courses remained on explaineracademy.com and became a significant contributor to our bottom line and fit with our style of business.

Looking back, the pieces fit together. The book was a relative success and it helped us feel more independent than ever. It introduced Common Craft to thousands of new people and our membership numbers grew consistently as people joined to access both videos and cut-outs. We weren't sure about the long-term impact of sharing our cut-outs, but we felt good about providing another resource that helped to solve our customers' problems. Then, we responded to customer requests by teaching video production via online courses that we developed ourselves.

And through it all, Common Craft remained the two-person, home-based business we set out to create.

THE TAKE HOMES:

→   If you have expertise, there may be business opportunities in helping others learn how to do what you do.

→   In sharing your knowledge, it may seem that you're creating competition. Don't let this stop you.

→   Lawyers are expensive. Educating people about how to use your work can be more productive than sending cease and desist letters.

→   When working through a new opportunity, take a step back and ask what biases you have regarding your partners and their input. Be prepared to change—the company may depend on it.

→   Writing a book can be a way to establish credibility and thought leadership. If you feel your perspective is useful to others, a book can help you stake your claim.

→   Consider how a book can contribute to your business and offer readers a reason to visit your website and engage in your work.

→   Look for byproducts that come from your work. Are you creating something as part of a bigger project that could have value on its own?

→   Public speaking is a skill that can only be improved through doing it. If you accept the challenge, you'll gain confidence quickly and have a new source of income that can help support your small business.

→   Online courses require upfront work, but can be attractive to customers and help you become a thought leader.

→   Rather than creating new brands and domains, consider building onto something you've already established.

10

Success
through Failure

ROWING UP, I always wanted to join my older brothers in whatever they were doing. They were teenagers when I was a little kid, so I never really fit in. They played Ping-Pong and I wanted to play too, despite being too young to truly compete. Part of the problem, in addition to being young, was that I was very respectful, maybe too respectful, of physical pain. I wanted to be a better athlete, but I feared hurting myself.

As I grew older and gained more skill, my brothers began to coach me a little more. I remember a specific time when they were trying to convince me to push a little harder and said, "Lee, if you're not falling down, you're not trying hard enough." It just wasn't in me to take those kinds of risks.

As an adult interested in business ideas, I saw a similar dynamic. The things I wanted to accomplish had inherent risks and required a bit of fortitude. While there wasn't any physical pain, the potential for failure was always present.

But unlike sports, it didn't seem to bother me. In fact, when developing Common Craft, the possibility of failure rarely entered my mind. Part of the reason is that I'm optimistic by nature. I have a deep well of hope. But I think it also had to do with what failure means to me in the context of business.

It's easy to think that failure in business means catastrophe. A business might go bankrupt, the investors and the founders might lose their money, layoffs could happen, and everyone will feel the pain. And it occurs regularly: Shikhar Ghosh at Harvard found that 75 percent of companies with venture capital funding never return money to investors, and 30–40 percent end up liquidating everything.

While that level of catastrophic failure happens, the most pervasive type of failure occurs every day. It's small scale, and it may sting and waste resources, but it also offers a lesson without costing you your life savings. As Thomas Edison famously said of inventing the lightbulb, "I have not failed. I've just found 10,000 ways that won't work."

This kind of failure could be an idea for a feature that never finds its way into production. It's an email campaign that doesn't produce results, or a price change that scares off customers. These failures are part of every entrepreneur's life, and learning to deal with them is part of improving a company's performance.

Once our membership service went live, it became a laboratory for testing ideas with a single metric: increasing memberships. Every day, I'd wake up thinking about ways we could move the needle. We would change the copy on the front page, rearrange the buttons by each video, or change the call to action at the end of each video. Sometimes we would work with developers to add a new feature, like enabling members to suggest and vote on video titles.

And most of the time, the idea didn't work well enough or we didn't implement it effectively. In this way, Common

Craft has constantly failed and every time, we have been unswayed. It felt like there was a perfect formula of features and messaging that could create a tsunami of memberships, and our job was to find it. We had to fail our way through and honestly, I came to see it as a fun element of our work. I became used to the fact that most ideas would fail, and took it as a challenge to have the next idea on deck. As we fiddled with Common Craft over many years, I sometimes found time to experiment on other projects.

An example was Kindle books. After the Amazon Kindle was released, the company offered a way for anyone to publish and sell books for the device. We loved the idea of self-publishing and created a dozen or so little Kindle books based on Common Craft videos. Instead of watching a video, you could buy a book for a couple of dollars and learn something new. I think we sold a handful of books.

Another example was a Common Craft app. I worked for months with an independent developer to create an early iPhone app that made it easy to watch Common Craft videos. The use case in my mind was people needing a way to explain technology on the go. I imagined a group of people trying to understand augmented reality, for example, and one person being able to pull out their phone and play a Common Craft video that would resolve the issue. It was early in the evolution of apps and it turned out to be a costly and wasteful endeavor that never made it to the App Store.

As Twitter was gaining momentum and our video was being used on their homepage, I became convinced that we could build a layer on top of Twitter that people would use to report the completion of tasks. I called it Task Love, and the idea was based on using peer pressure as motivation. I built it with the help of contractors, but it never went anywhere.

There are a few common threads in these failures. First, they were projections of my hubris. Because Common

Craft videos had produced attention and relative success, I believed that I possessed a skill that could be applied to other projects. It felt like success was somehow inevitable, or the attention we received from the videos could be converted to other products. For the most part, this was not true. Second, they were not good businesses or products. I had no evidence that anyone wanted a Common Craft Kindle book or app. They produced little to no income and required hours to produce and/or maintain. Of course, this was the case with the first Common Craft videos and they eventually produced income, so that may have been an influence. Third, they were wasteful. At the time, I was not thinking in terms of ROI. I never calculated how much income the idea would need to generate to cover the development and operational costs. I spent serious time and money on the projects and got very little out of them compared to how that time and money could have been spent on our core products.

Sachi, for her part, was not all that supportive of these side projects. She saw that they were not good product ideas and worked to sway my attention and direct my focus to our videos. But at the same time, she could see how passionate I was about them. They animated me and filled some part of me that needed to keep pushing. I am easily seduced by the potential to create something new.

It's hard to feel regretful because I was trying. They were wasteful ideas and not likely to succeed, but not catastrophic failures. I was learning and getting accustomed to the feeling that most ideas aren't wildly successful, and that part of being an entrepreneur is maintaining a sense of hope. The formula for real success is out there somewhere, and the path to finding it is littered with failures big and small. If you're not failing, you're not trying hard enough.

In 2014, we had to face another kind of failure. Since 2008, we'd managed the Explainer Network, which was a simple marketplace for matching leads with video producers. In the two years after our first video, the Explainer Network represented a significant portion of the producers serving the burgeoning market for explainer videos. But over time, it started to flag.

The idea of explainer videos went mainstream and anyone with animation skills suddenly started claiming they were producing explainer videos, too. For most of these producers, the label "explainer" was just a marketing term or a way to repackage the same mediocre demos and advertisements they were producing otherwise. In my perception, most of these producers were not focused on clarity but selling. Explainer videos, as a concept, were being eaten by the advertising beast.

Next, producers from around the world started jumping into the explainer video market and offering "explainer videos" for a fraction of the cost. These new competitors changed the market and created confusion when compared to the work being performed by Explainer Network producers and Common Craft. A serious, results-focused explainer video could cost tens of thousands of dollars and take months to complete. This stood in stark contrast to producers in developing nations claiming to produce similar videos for $500. People who needed a video started to ask, "Why would I pay so much for something I can get for a few hundred dollars?" All I could say was, "You get what you pay for."

Eventually, the market changed in fundamental ways. The Explainer Network members, facing a decision about where to find their next custom video clients, had a choice to stay or go. After all, it was a marketplace and they weren't locked in. After years of success, Explainer Network members started to bow out, despite increased traffic from the book. We went from nine members to six and then after a while, down to four or five. This meaningful data was constantly on my mind. I wanted to help, but the market forces seemed too powerful.

We had a choice. We could invest more in the network and try to keep it viable through spending money on advertising, or we could just let it go. Rather than fighting the current, we decided to go with the flow, and that meant closing it down. In 2014, we sent an email to the remaining members saying that the Explainer Network was officially closed. A company called Splainers, which was one of the original Explainer Network members, became our long-standing primary partner in serving the demand for high-quality explainer videos.

Seeing the Explainer Network fold was a good reminder that few business ideas last through changing markets. Constant renewal is often required to keep them going. Needs change, tools evolve, trends emerge. I couldn't help but feel a little satisfaction that we'd chosen, years before, to move out of the custom video market. The world that birthed Common Craft as a consulting practice was gone and with it, the environment that led to our videos being popular. This new landscape of viral YouTube videos meant that we were no longer special or recognized. The internet, collectively, had moved on and we couldn't depend on buzz.

It was ironic because, early on, many people saw us as experts in social media. Having come from early experience in online communities and blogging, I was seen as someone with deep experience. And for a while, I considered myself an expert. But that changed as I started to realize that the requirements of social media success had evolved. Being a producer of unique explainer videos was no longer enough to get attention. To earn a growing audience, you had to be provocative, fully engaged, and willing to devote serious time and effort. The wide-scale adoption of social media had surpassed me and my skills, and it wasn't in me to work toward the modern version of social media fame.

While I admire those who compete in the crowded world of Instagram, TikTok, Snapchat, and YouTube, I get enormous satisfaction in seeing success from a different perspective. More than ever, we saw ourselves as educators who were 100 percent devoted to serving the needs of our members and users of our products. Rather than working for fame, views, likes, and recognition, we're focused on keeping Common Craft members happy, making videos that solve a problem, and running a business that contributes to our well-being.

Along with the market for explainer videos, video production tools were changing and taking the explainer video market in new directions. One of those businesses was GoAnimate (now called Vyond) which was growing quickly and attracting global attention. GoAnimate's product is an inexpensive, do-it-yourself method for creating animated videos using a web browser. Anyone with an internet connection can log on to their website and create videos by dragging characters and props into scenes and animating them to match a voice-over.

In seeing this trend, we asked the same question we did when other producers started making explainer videos: *is this a threat or an opportunity? Do we fight against it, or find opportunities in going with the flow?* As with the Explainer Network and copycats, we chose to see it as an opportunity and a new way to earn revenue. With custom videos on the back burner and Common Craft membership humming along, we had time to experiment. We also had a growing library of digital cut-outs that we owned and could use as a resource. What if Common Craft cut-outs were also available inside these platforms? And, of course, what if it worked?

Unlike most of our previous strategies, this direction would require business development, which took the form of me contacting potential partners and pitching the idea of working together. If my pitch worked, we'd need to work out pricing and how Common Craft media are stored and presented on third-party websites. It was uncharted territory for us, but I was excited because it fit so perfectly into our way of doing business. It didn't require additional employees, an office, overhead, or travel. Once everything was in place, the cut-outs could reach a much wider audience and we could receive monthly income by simply having our cut-outs on another company's website. Further, these relationships meant our income could continue to grow passively.

We considered this strategy a distribution model. By working with distributors, we could reach much larger markets. We worked with partners to offer our videos and cut-outs to their members in exchange for a share of revenue or a monthly licensing fee. The main risk we saw in pursuing distribution is cannibalization. The customers would not be ours to serve and support in the future, so there was a potential to reduce Common Craft membership. We were willing to take this risk as the Common Craft website would always remain the home of our work. More than ever, we relied on the power of ownership. Distribution was only possible because we decided in 2007 to keep producing original videos and cut-outs and retaining the copyright. Had we stopped making original videos and focused on the short bet of custom videos, we wouldn't have owned anything that we could distribute or license.

To get started, I contacted GoAnimate and asked about the potential of adding Common Craft cut-outs to their platform. The GoAnimate founder had contacted us previously and I knew they would likely be interested in talking. Within a day or so the company's CEO wrote back to say they were big fans of Common Craft and would be happy to talk. Over the next year we worked out an agreement where Common Craft cut-outs would live inside GoAnimate and be available as an upgrade to any account. We shared the resulting revenue, and Common Craft now had a new monthly income stream.

This scenario repeated multiple times over the next couple years. The Common Craft brand was our ambassador, opening doors and starting conversations. It didn't matter that we were a two-person, home-based business. We were Common Craft and that meant something greater than the two of us. Sometimes a partner like TechSmith would sell a pack of 2,000 cut-outs on their website. Other times, a partner like eLearning Brothers would resell our video and cut-out libraries. In one case, Common Craft videos became part of a large membership service for educators. In all these examples, there was a long period of negotiation and technical integration, followed by the result: monthly or quarterly checks arriving automatically. As with the first time we sold a video download, it was magical to receive this mailbox money—and a clear sign that our plan was working.

The distribution partners helped fill the hole left by the Explainer Network. We had mutually beneficial relationships that lasted for years. But, over time, business evolved as it always does. Two of our biggest partners changed their models after a couple of years and our partnership was done. My lesson in working on these partnerships is that they have great potential. They can produce passive income over the long term. But they require time to set up and the relationships are usually unpredictable. Without warning an email could arrive with news of changing business models that don't include our products. All we could do is say, "We had a good run" and keep pushing. It's another kind of platform risk.

As we approached the tenth anniversary of publishing our first video, burnout was starting to take a toll. The constant weight of always producing original videos started to feel like a burden, even though we'd designed Common Craft around growing that product. Having seen our business's models come and go, I started to wonder if we were destined to make original videos forever. At one point, I even floated the idea of getting the library to 100 titles and then taking a break. Other income streams were doing well and the library was big enough to be self-sustaining. I thought it was time to reevaluate how we felt about making more videos over the long term. Where would we draw the line? Is there a point at which it becomes time to consider what's next?

Sachi took a dim view of this possibility. The videos led to reliable revenue, and were the biggest reason people joined Common Craft. Plus, publishing new videos every month created an incentive for our members to keep renewing their annual memberships. And I wanted to stop making them? Ha.

Amid this frustration, I started looking for alternatives to the heavyweight production method we'd developed. Despite refining our production process over many years, it was still time-consuming to bring a Common Craft video to life, especially in the production phase. Once a script and storyboard were finalized, we had to cut out hundreds of pieces of paper, film them on a whiteboard using stop-motion animation, and edit the video to match a voice-over in order to achieve the effect people knew as a Common Craft Style video. While shooting a video only took half a day, the entire process could take forty to seventy hours per video.

I couldn't help but wonder if our videos could evolve just like the company. What if we changed our production method in fundamental ways? This question caused me to take another look at the essentials of a Common Craft video.

The style of our stop-motion animation was simple. The cut-outs appeared, disappeared, and moved across the screen. Using live video footage meant we could use human hands in the frame, but were those required?

These questions led to a period of experimentation that was governed by constraints. We wanted to find a more streamlined method for creating original videos that still felt like Common Craft. Whatever form it took, it would have to use the same visuals, the same voice-over, and the same approach to explanation.

Having created many presentations with both Power-Point and Keynote, I started to experiment with their built-in animation features. I could add a cut-out to a slide and animate it much like in our videos. The images could appear, move, disappear, et cetera. I didn't need to learn professional animation tools to create animations that matched our videos. I was amazed at how simple it could be.

Soon it was all I wanted to work on. As a test, I recreated scenes from existing videos using cut-outs and animation features in presentation software. These tests showed that Common Craft videos could be animated with amazing consistency and in about half the time. This innovation was in line with how we wanted to evolve. Cutting out hundreds of pieces of paper and shooting stop-motion scenes were not a great use of our time and expertise. By going digital, we could move past this production process and make room for putting our real skills to work in the form of clear explanations.

By the end of 2017, little Common Craft had experimented with several business models, partnerships, and arrangements. We had earned income through numerous streams:

- Consulting
- Custom video projects
- Licensing videos
- Licensing cut-outs
- Memberships (videos and cut-outs)
- Distribution and partner agreements
- Referrals/revenue sharing for video projects
- Book advance and royalties
- Speaking engagements
- Online courses

This list reads like a collection of successes, and to some degree, it's true. They each represent a strategy that worked. But what's missing is all the failures and missed opportunities. You can't see the effort, debate, and constant revision it took to make them work. They are all a product of the small-scale, everyday frustration and failure that is required to keep pushing and evolving. Together, these diversified revenue streams fed the fire. While all the models produced income, we focused on the ones that resulted in the shareholder value we designed Common Craft to produce: the ability to have a choice in how we spend our time. We could do it all and then some, while remaining two people working from home.

THE TAKE HOMES:

→ If you're not failing, you're not trying hard enough.

→ No business is immune to failure and it can happen quickly when markets change. Stay focused on the big picture of your industry. When change happens, be prepared to evolve.

→ Most business ideas fail in one form or another. Get used to seeing failure as a necessary element of success. Accept the challenge and keep hope alive.

→ Building new things is fun and exciting, but it can also be wasteful. Don't get distracted. Stay focused on your core offering.

→ When you see change happening, don't assume it's a threat. Be open to reaching out to potential partners and creating new relationships that extend your reach.

The Power
Not to Care

FAMOUS ANECDOTE FROM Greek history is the story
of Alexander the Great and Diogenes, a philosopher
known for his simple lifestyle. While many versions
of the story exist, the version told by Plutarch goes something like this:

Alexander, a respected prince at the time, was in Corinth
and visited Diogenes. He expected Diogenes to congratulate
him or request something of him, as most did. Alexander
found Diogenes lying leisurely in the sun. Diogenes was star-
tled to see Alexander and his entourage. Alexander asked if
he needed anything and Diogenes replied, "Yes, stand a little
out of my sun." Alexander was taken aback by this honest
response from the philosopher, who obviously did not care
about Alexander's standing or power. As Alexander and his
men were about to walk away, Alexander said, "But truly, if
I were not Alexander, I wish I were Diogenes."

I first read this anecdote in an essay by Tim Kreider
called "Power? No, Thanks, I'm Good." Kreider is an essayist

and cartoonist who often writes about his unconventional interpretations of success, power, and time. "I would define power as the ability to make other people do what you want; freedom is the ability to do what you want," he writes. He then goes on to ask, "Who was ultimately more powerful: the conqueror Alexander, who ruled the known world, or the philosopher Diogenes, whom Alexander could neither offer nor threaten with anything?"

In short, power can take many forms. Alexander's kind of power seems logical, and can be applied to entrepreneurship. A leader's skills and ambitions are used to command armies of employees and a growing organization that's capable of overcoming fierce competition. This power runs the engine of capitalism, which rewards constant growth and increasing shareholder value.

The other kind of power is that of Diogenes, which comes from no one being able to tell you what to do or think or how to use your time. It's a modest kind of power, but one that holds incredible potential; after all, even Alexander saw its appeal. It's the power of freedom from the expectations of others and of society at large.

Ever since Adam Smith explained market forces and built the foundation of capitalism, the assumption has been that you had to run a business like Alexander. You had to grow and conquer. You had to exploit every opportunity to build market share, crush the competition, and produce shareholder value. While this approach to business isn't perfect, it works. It has produced inventions and innovations that changed the world, like the telephone. It helped to lift millions out of poverty by providing jobs with steady wages. We need Alexanders who are powerful and prepared to take on the responsibility of managing growing businesses with armies of employees.

But is it the only way?

What we discovered in experimenting with Common Craft for over a decade was that it's also possible to build a business that's more in line with Diogenes's form of power, which values independence and flexibility. It means making a deliberate choice in how you measure success and perceive happiness. It means being able to tell people like Alexander to buzz off.

Businesses have always existed that were more like Diogenes. The owners of an intentionally small business can earn a good living, do meaningful work, support a family, and adhere to a lifestyle that suits them. Their ambition may be more focused on home or family than growing and conquering, and there is real power and satisfaction in that pursuit.

Now, I don't mean to infer that Diogenes is a hero of business or that entrepreneurs should emulate an ancient philosopher whose reputation in history is more complicated than it appears in this story. He is simply a symbol of the idea that entrepreneurship does not have to take the form of Alexander and his army. Though we didn't realize it at the time, we built Common Craft so that we could be more like Diogenes. We made deliberate decisions that reduced our potential to build traditional power and income, and increased our potential to have more control of our time and lives. We realized that our success didn't depend on dominating markets as much as serving a relatively small group of dedicated customers and a willingness to remain flexible and evolve over time.

By making this our goal, we had to accept that we'd never be known as "real" entrepreneurs.

Why would a "real" entrepreneur want to run a business that's intentionally small? It's a valid question and my answer has less to do with the size of a company and more to do with what makes an entrepreneur "real." As Jason Fried and David Heinemeier Hansson wrote in their book *Rework*, the word "entrepreneur" comes with baggage. "It smells of a members-only club," they write. "Everyone should be encouraged to start his own business, not just some rare breed that self-identifies as an entrepreneur."

What I've learned is when the goal is to prove oneself, there is no business or salary big enough. It's like a video game. As soon as one level of success is reached, the next level appears with new, more powerful foes. The game never ends, and many entrepreneurs spend their lives playing it, in part, because they're driven to win. And in most cases, winning means amassing the most money and recognition.

In an interview with Matt D'Avella, Paul Jarvis, author of *Company of One*, described a situation where he had a goal of making a million dollars in a year. He soon realized that he was working so hard that he couldn't enjoy having the money and didn't really see how more money would make his life better. He started to reconsider why he was chasing that goal. He saw that businesspeople are often motivated to create what they see as a legitimate business, which includes opening an office, hiring employees, or making a certain amount of money. He asked himself, "Are you running the business for yourself or are you running it for the way it looks to other people?"

It's easy to get trapped in the perspective that your business success is relative to others, and that the same few data points apply to every business owner. We saw this dynamic many times when we used to attend tech conferences and found ourselves having the same conversations over and over. Everyone's company is the next big thing. They are prepared with talking points about how many employees they've hired, how much investment they've received from venture capitalists or angel investors, and the next product that's coming out of beta. And I get it. It is the currency of the realm.

When the conversation turned to me in these situations, I could talk about Common Craft videos and they would often remember our work. In their minds, we were creative people uninterested in business or "real" entrepreneurship. They assumed our passion was video production and we probably got hired to make custom videos, which was true. Learning we are a two-person company only buttressed that perspective. In the tech world, we *couldn't* really matter because we didn't have an army of employees and millions of dollars in investment. And in a traditional business environment, that perspective is often accurate. If you develop a successful product, hire a team, and beat the competition, you can win—it's no wonder these factors have become a way to evaluate success. What you don't hear is the daily reality of running these businesses and what it's like to wake up every morning thinking about how much of someone else's money is being spent on an idea that may or may not work.

In the context of a conversation in the hallway of a tech conference, I rarely had a chance to explain that, yes, our work is creative, but we are entrepreneurs too. We're just playing a different game. We may not have 100 employees, but I haven't had a meeting in three weeks. We may not have vc funding, but I haven't used an alarm clock in years. We may not have a board of directors, but I earn passive income from my home office.

Coming to this understanding wasn't easy, especially for me. From the very beginning of our work together, Sachi has championed the idea that there is value in ignoring what others think about you and your business; instead, consider how solving a problem and satisfying customers can lead to what you really want. I have never met anyone who is more focused on creating her own path. Throughout Sachi's life, expectations and obligations felt like a burden or an obstacle to be overcome. They held her back and prevented her from being in control and having the freedom to explore her options. Learning about her commitment to this perspective surprised me and made me question my own path. Was I doing what I really wanted, or was I outsourcing that to the expectation of others?

Sachi taught me that it was okay to play an active role in challenging what was expected, or actively avoiding it. And for a while, I wasn't sure how to react. Living according to expectations gave me comfort, even if I couldn't explain why. While I still have a traditional side, I've now come to revel in the idea that I have the power to decide how my time is used and that no one's expectations can interfere with the path I want to take, unless I want them to.

When Common Craft videos came along, it took time to figure out how to think about the business in the context of expectations. We had a number of opportunities before us and could have built the business according to what business culture says you're supposed to do. We could have gone the traditional, expected route.

Our thinking started to change when Sachi and I realized that the goal of legitimacy in the eyes of others was a trap that could come with consequences. You might earn the respect and admiration of your peers, but at what cost? Are you willing to trade happiness and flexibility for it?

With Sachi's help, I adjusted my thinking. I learned to let go of what other people thought and to take pride in the decisions we made and the business we built. I learned to appreciate that Common Craft reflects us and what we want out of life. If the business didn't support the lives we wanted to lead, then what's it all for?

A few years ago, an article in *The Guardian* captured the "Top Five Regrets of the Dying" as told to Bronnie Ware, a palliative care nurse, by terminal patients. This was number one on the list:

> I wish I'd had the courage to live a life true to myself, not the life others expected of me.

When people realize their life is almost over and look back with clarity, it's easy to see how many dreams have gone unfulfilled. With this in mind, it's my hope that you will look at your life and ask yourself what has influenced your path and what might determine it in the future. You might find there are opportunities to make decisions that will shape the life you want to lead or create for those around you. You have more choices than you realize, and the first step is considering what it means to be true to yourself and how you use your time.

I realize that this perspective can seem selfish because it's focused on personal time and lifestyle, but I also think there is plenty of room for both selfishness and selflessness. Being in control of your life and building a business that supports it can promote a more selfless style of living. It can mean being more available for family and friends. It can mean time to volunteer and to be a more productive part of a community. As the research shows, living in service to others and something greater than yourself is a path to maximizing the 40 percent of happiness that's in your control.

Taking control of your life and your time often requires trade-offs and sacrifices. In order to achieve it, you may have to live the monetorium and be conscious of every penny you spend. You may have to say "no" to opportunities and leave some money on the table because, if those opportunities work and grow, you may not remain in control for long. But if you are successful, you can finally feel the freedom that comes with no one being able to tell you what to do.

THE TAKE HOMES:

→   Not every business has to grow and conquer. It is possible to design a business to be small and achieve power through autonomy.

→   This new form of business comes with different measures of success that are based more on lifestyle and flexibility than brimming bank accounts and jam-packed schedules.

→   A company that's "Big Enough" by your standards may not earn respect from other entrepreneurs who don't get it. Forget about them. You're playing a different game with different outcomes.

→   The expectations of society and the business world can feel overwhelming. There is constant pressure to do what you're "supposed" to do and run a business the way it's "supposed" to be run. Learn to ignore it.

→   Designing a business to support the lifestyle you want comes with trade-offs and sacrifices. Hard work, long timelines, and an acceptance of risk may be required. There are no shortcuts.

Conclusion

Big Satisfaction
on a Small Island

U P TO NOW, I've focused on describing Common Craft, but I haven't really discussed our lifestyle and what it's like to run a home-based business with a spouse. I'd like to jump to the present and share what has become the biggest project of our lives.

Over the last couple of years, I've finally let myself believe that our lives have changed and we've reached the goal that we set out to achieve so many years ago. We are finally Big Enough. For so long, I felt that we were close, but things were still tenuous enough that it felt too good to be true. I feared we were living in a dream and that, at some point, we'd wake up, just as it became too late to correct our course.

Sachi has always been a believer. As our de facto CFO, the reality of the business and our financial situation is part of her everyday life and she has always had confidence that we were, and still are, on the right track. When I suspect the numbers are low, she's there with a spreadsheet and graph that shows where we are and where we expect to be. There are flush months and slow months, and that's all part of business.

Despite designing Common Craft to work without being connected to our time and effort, our goal has never been to stop working. We work a full-time load. What we wanted was for work to be something that fit us, something we controlled, creatively, logistically, and fiscally. It's this sense of control that leads to our happiness at work and hopefully translates into happy Common Craft members.

Today, we are continuing to experiment as our video library grows. Recently, we introduced a new "streaming" plan that is monthly and designed for educators along with anyone interested in learning about technology and the internet. As our library has evolved, we've become more focused on helping people use the web with confidence. These videos explain subjects related to digital responsibility and internet safety.

In nearly every part of the company, Sachi and I play consistent roles. Working together, we agree on a course of action and the outcome we want. Then, I take the lead creating the first draft and send it to her for editing when it feels ready. From that point, we iterate until it's finished. This is true for explainer video scripts and storyboards, plans for new features, webinar presentations, and even emails. Nearly everything is a team effort and it works because we bring different skills to the table.

For over a decade, producing new original Common Craft videos has been a constant project. These days, we work on them in batches of three and I usually start the process by looking through suggestions from our members and doing a bit of research on topics that seem to be relevant.

Then, I propose a few titles and we talk through what we feel would be the best additions to the video library. We ask, "What needs a better explanation?" I research the subjects and write a rough draft of a video script and share it with Sachi. From this point, we pass it back and forth as the script changes constantly and sometimes drastically, all the way until the voice-over is recorded. The script is the heart of a Common Craft video and we take time to get it right. Sometimes, that means asking subject matter experts to provide feedback and validate our approach.

Having worked in this manner for a decade, it seems normal. I couldn't imagine it any other way. I need Sachi's editing and direction and she needs my starting point. Thankfully, we are very different people with different skills that happen to overlap in productive ways. I am not very detail-oriented, and Sachi is very much so. I am creative and she is analytical. It works because we have a shared vision of what we're trying to accomplish. Usually, the destination is clear and agreed upon. We decide to take on a project and until it's complete, it's our primary focus. We put everything into it. It could be a new Explainer Academy course, a newsletter issue, or a set of cut-outs. There is always another project on the horizon.

Each morning begins in the same way. I am usually awake by 7 a.m. thanks to my internal clock. Part of me wishes I could sleep later, but I can't. I flip back the covers as our dogs, Maybe and Piper, jump onto the bed to ensure I keep moving. They are both Bernedoodles, which is a mix of standard poodle and Bernese mountain dog. Together, they represent over 100 pounds of canine that always seem to be starving in the mornings.

Once I'm up, I head straight to the coffee maker and set it to "Brew," give the dogs their breakfast, and take them out for a quick walk. Upon returning, they race to the bedroom and pounce on Sachi, whose internal clock would allow for an hour more sleep if not for the dogs.

On a typical morning, I have between ten and twenty emails in my inbox and most don't need attention. Over time, I have learned to keep email under control and having more than twenty emails in my inbox gives me stress. The only kind of email that really matters to us is from Common Craft members.

Usually, I don't have meetings. Without employees, investors, custom video clients, vendors, or partners, there isn't much of a need. And working from home means I only meet online anyway. It's been years since I walked into a corporate meeting room. The meetings I do have are usually with designers or developers and focus on something new, like a feature for our website.

My day is entirely self-directed and that sometimes means that I'm not working at all. Part of having control of our time means that we can choose to get errands done or leave town when other people are at work. We can choose to avoid rush hour traffic and long lines at Costco. These choices don't replace work hours, just shift them. A Wednesday spent running errands is accounted for by work on a Saturday or a quiet Thursday evening.

Our reality, for better or for worse, is that work never ends. Even while having a picnic dinner with wine and a sunset, we're likely to talk about work more than anything else. To some, that may sound like the least romantic thing possible, but for us, it is romantic. We are talking about something we love and something we're accomplishing together. We can discuss. We can celebrate. We can dream.

The work that fills our days is often a mix of things we enjoy and things that are required. We are the support staff, the janitors, and the bookkeepers. We write every newsletter, every blog post, every tweet, and personally respond to every email. Outside of web development, we do it all and constantly search for ways to make it all work together.

I like to work in a typical, ergonomically designed office environment in our home. I have a desk, a proper office chair, and a laptop workstation with a Wacom tablet I use for creating Common Craft artwork. Sachi, on the other hand, works anywhere but the office. This often means on the couch, in our living room chairs, and even in bed. The bed sometimes wins because the dogs can join her. While we mostly work from home, it's not required. We can and do work from anywhere with an internet connection, but home is usually our favorite.

For me, not having a normal workplace can get a little lonely. There is no water cooler gossip or work friends to meet for lunch. I don't feel part of a team and I sometimes miss that feeling of being part of a bigger organization. I would probably enjoy managing a team in the right circumstance, but I'm not willing to trade our independence for it.

As much as I want to be the freewheeling person who is unconcerned with keeping traditional work hours, I have learned that I am just not that person. Even with all the control in the world, I am still drawn to working a normal 9-to-5 day from the comfort of home. I get real satisfaction from the feeling of a hard day's work, even as Sachi pushes me to take advantage of our lifestyle and be free from tradition, like her.

A couple of years ago, when we felt that Common Craft had become the company we wanted, we looked for ways to exercise our independence. If we could live and work from anywhere, why not go? Over the next year, we created a plan to drive across the country, with our dogs, to Charleston, South Carolina, where we'd live and work for three months and then drive back to Seattle. And that's what we did. In

Charleston we created courses for the Explainer Academy, which proved to me that we were, in fact, as independent as we had hoped.

Right now, our lives are more turbulent than they've ever been because we are working on a project that will lay the foundation for the next phase of our lives. We've never anticipated anything so much and the happiness we feel is real.

This project began two years ago when we went camping on Orcas Island, where I wrote *The Art of Explanation*. We'd visited Orcas consistently since our first weekend away together twenty years earlier. On this trip, we arrived early and decided to kill time by peeking at real estate listings. On a whim, we walked into an office and had someone print out flyers for vacant land.

At the time, we figured we couldn't afford a nice house in addition to our Seattle home and that vacant land could be a way to reserve our island spot for the future. That night we drank wine out of a box by the campfire and talked endlessly about what it would be like to own property on the island and someday, live there. It seemed like the logical evolution of the lifestyle we'd tried to create for ourselves over the previous twelve years. It was exciting to consider but still seemed more like a drunken dream.

Over the following days and weeks, the dream didn't fade and we found ourselves back at Orcas Island, this time with a realtor. Before we knew it, we'd stumbled upon a property that we didn't think was possible in our price range. It had a strange, yurt-shaped house on it that a family built from a kit in the '80s. More importantly, it had a view over the water. It was the first and only house we toured, and we jumped at it.

At first, we stayed weekends, and then weeks at a time. We grew to love the location and the island itself, which punches far above its weight when it comes to natural beauty, and amenities like restaurants and cultural activities. Orcas is a popular tourist destination, and for good reason. It's part of an archipelago called the San Juan Islands that is known for wildlife, water-based activities, and charming seaside towns.

There are a few thousand permanent residents and a surprising number of like-minded people. We quickly found a community and felt at home. As someone described it when we first arrived, "Orcas is like a small town, but with an open mind."

It felt like a luxury to have an island home to entertain friends who visited, and it was. But as we split our time, it started to create drag in our lives. We started to feel that, instead of one whole life, we had two half-lives and our relationships were suffering. Plus, it was expensive and added a layer of maintenance to a lifestyle that was designed to be lightweight.

Early on, Sachi started to express the idea that maybe Orcas Island was becoming our home and at first I didn't feel the same. But soon I started to change. My first indication was when we would make ferry reservations for going back to Seattle. As that date approached, I felt a sense of dread. I wanted to stay on the island for just a little longer.

Eventually, we both agreed. Orcas Island would be home. This decision set into motion a series of events that saw us sell the house in Seattle we'd owned since 2003 and move to Orcas Island as permanent residents. In the past year, we have moved from Seattle to the yurt-shaped house and from there to a 500-square-foot guesthouse over a neighbor's garage. That's where I finished this book.

The yurt-shaped house was small, dilapidated, and not the kind of house one uses as the foundation for the future. Its fifteen-sided shape meant renovation options were few and far between. Over the past eighteen months, we've worked with an architect friend to design a new house that will be our forever home and Common Craft's global headquarters. The house design project became, after our normal work, the focus of our daily lives. We took advantage of our flexibility to balance work and the needs of the architect and builders. We both love the process of thinking through home design. Common Craft allowed us to devote time to get the plans right while taking care of the business.

Like many parts of Washington State, Orcas Island has a wide variety of homes and as we were designing ours, we paid close attention. Many of the nicer houses were built by people who were retiring and moving to the island with savings to spend on a large home. There are many three- and four-story homes with numerous bedrooms. It seems like the intention was to be big and make a statement through sheer volume. The houses were a symbol of power and having made it—like the business they owned, or the income they earned.

It struck me that our home design, like our business, could also be Big Enough and we had a choice. For example, we could use cheaper materials and a simpler design to build a bigger house. Or, we could use the same money on the quality and design of a smaller house that's easier to manage. I probably don't have to tell you what we chose.

Our approach to this design meant using constraints to define what was important to us and give the house a cohesive feel. It needed to be a single story, which accounted for the accessibility we may need in the future. It needed to feed, sleep, and entertain up to six adults at a time. The house will have three bedrooms, one of which doubles as my office, and a design that maximizes the view. It will be very efficient and sized for our needs and not the expectations of others.

While building the house is a big project to manage, the real change that we feel is more personal. In moving to Orcas, we've committed to change. The longer we're on the island, the more we can see that the culture fits with the lives we want to lead. Practicality and self-sufficiency are an indelible part of island living. For most, it is a simpler life with simpler pleasures, and at this stage in our lives, that feels right.

Last summer was the first time we got a real glimpse of what was possible. We became dedicated crabbers and over the summer, caught over eighty Dungeness crabs. A neighbor has a large garden and kept our kitchen full of lettuce, squash, zucchini, carrots, asparagus, and more. We rarely had dinner out and when we did, it was often a dive bar burger, which made me happy. Slowly but surely, we shed expenses that we had accumulated in Seattle for things like parking, train tickets, and events. At the moment, our non-construction expenses are lower than they've ever been, mainly because we no longer live in the city. Viva la monetorium!

At the same time, we have grown to be part of the community. Despite being small, Orcas attracts interesting people who come to the island for similar reasons. They're ready for change and more practical living. We often find ourselves sitting around campfires and enjoying dinner at potlucks. We take boat rides and hikes with friends. It was at these events that we realized we'd escaped the Seattle bubble. The discussions were not about corporate jobs but farming, fishing, and small-town scuttlebutt.

Once the house is complete and we can get back to a more normal living situation, we expect to continue to live with low expenses and waste very little. In fact, our goal is to live with as much self-sufficiency as reasonably possible. And we'll have help. Orcas Island is full of self-sufficiency role models.

I don't want to give the impression that we're going to check out of society and live off the grid in the woods. Far from it. The house will be comfortable, modern, and built to last. We will remain connected and engaged, but we'll be doing it from a place that allows us to enjoy the outdoors, the quiet, and the potential to slow down. The property has a well, a septic system, and a propane tank, with plans for solar power and a substantial garden. Along with fishing and crabbing, it's possible to live, to a surprising degree, off the land and water. That, to me, sounds like a dream.

We will, of course, continue to work on Common Craft and I plan to stay as busy as ever. In fact, I recently added a new layer to our work in the form of a personal newsletter called "Ready for Rain." I made it a goal to publish a new essay every week for a year and it has been a chance for me to connect with friends and family along with practicing my writing.

Throughout the book, you've seen my focus on the future. I try to keep an eye out for what's next and how change might create new opportunities. Together, Sachi and I have honed that sense and it led me to quit my job and start consulting just as online communities were emerging as a business tool. It led us to create videos about social media tools and put them on YouTube just as people started to adopt them. It led us to discover new ways to earn a living from our original videos. The list goes on.

When I look around, I see people who are busy and have very little control over their lives or their time. Every moment is filled and for some, that's a choice. But this busyness seems to be becoming the new normal. It's easy to confuse being busy with being productive and engaged. It seems like self-worth gets wrapped into being busy every second of the day and it's become a strange badge of honor. From my perspective, it's not sustainable and arguably, not healthy.

At the same time, I see new ideas emerging about what it means to live the "good life" and often, it's focused on having and doing less, not more. Orcas Island and many places like it are playing a new role in the lives of professionals who have found, thanks to increased connectivity and permissive workplaces, that work can happen from almost anywhere. And often, a change of context can go a long way to getting their lives under control.

In the city, it seemed like we were always in a hurry. Something as simple as meeting friends for happy hour could turn into a stressful planning session. We might push to finish work so we could avoid rush hour traffic. Were the Mariners or Seahawks playing or was there construction to detour around? Ugh, the traffic. Can we find a parking spot in that neighborhood or should we walk to the train? Maybe an Uber or Car 2 Go can get us there? And this was just for a simple happy hour. Gridlock starts to feel normal.

When we first arrived on the island, I found myself continuing to rush, like some vestige of Seattle life was clinging to me and pushing me through tasks. The pressure made the muscles in my back and shoulders feel tense like they did in Seattle traffic. Then one day, I realized that something had fundamentally changed. There was no rush hour or competition for parking spaces. It took me a while to get used to the idea that I could slow down and savor taking my time. I grew to love making a fire in a wood stove and tending it over an evening. I looked forward to slow cooking food on the grill and learning that it's okay to do nothing. There is magic in eating a home-cooked meal and tuning out for the evening.

When we first moved to Orcas Island, we became friends with our next-door neighbors. Grant and his wife, Kathy, have lived on the island for twenty-five years and he is a never-ending source of anecdotes about island life. On multiple occasions he's said, "You'll see, it's different here. And it'll add twenty-five years to your life." That sounds like the place I want to be.

Epilogue
Defining "Big Enough" for Yourself

'VE TOLD THE story of creating a business and lifestyle that's Big Enough for us. Now it's your turn. Let's define what "Big Enough" means for you, and how you can apply the lessons we've learned over the years.

Big Enough, at heart, is about taking control of your life and choosing to follow a path that is focused on your values and your happiness. It's about realizing that constant growth, whether it's your company or your assets, isn't required and may create drag that prevents you from discovering happiness in parts of your life that support your values.

Our story of being Big Enough is unique and reflects what we value, like flexibility and control of our time. Your story may be very different and that's an important point in understanding Big Enough. We all have different values and beliefs about what makes us happy. The key is not following a list of rules, but realizing that you have a choice and that it's possible to design your life or your business around the values that matter to you.

For example, a software developer with aging parents may choose to only take on projects that can be done remotely, so being a part-time caregiver can be possible. A successful executive may decide on the job with a shorter commute to be able to exercise in the mornings. Or an entrepreneur may invest in keeping current customers happy instead of doubling sales each quarter. In all of these cases, values lead the way.

To entrepreneurs, this might sound at first like a lazy approach to business. Big Enough doesn't seem like a goal for an ambitious businessperson or a path to success. That is part of the problem. Success can be defined in numerous ways and ambition can take many forms and produce many outcomes. Who's to say that the ultimate goal has to be connected with ever-increasing wealth and assets? Can ambition not manifest in other ways? What's the end product of your ambition?

When we were trying to figure out the future of Common Craft, I felt we were being very ambitious by choosing to take a risk that allowed us to remain a small company. Further, we knew that if the bet paid off, we'd have a kind of success that was rare. We could have enough money, be wealthy with time, and have absolute control of our lives.

I believe it's time to think differently about what it means to be successful in business and as a professional. While money, assets, and number of employees will always matter, I believe there is room for people who see success through the lens of their personal values. You may not have a corner office and a mega-yacht, but you have time to go camping, attend little league games, and have dinner with loved ones every night. You can live in a location that you choose. You can follow your passions and pursue what makes you happy. To me, that's the healthy way to think about success: living according to one's values.

It may seem like the Big Enough approach is based on seeing money as a problem. But money absolutely matters and is an essential part of gaining control of your life. As I discussed in chapter 4, money is a major source of happiness up to the point when needs are met. Once that threshold is crossed, however, it starts to lose its happiness-promoting power. This is true for both entrepreneurs and corporate employees. Money matters, but comes with diminishing returns. If it grows too much, it can become a burden.

The question becomes, how do you know how much money is enough?

The answer to this question comes down to good old-fashioned financial responsibility. In order to think through what Big Enough means to you or your business, your financial house needs to be in order. For individuals, this means you've achieved a traditional form of success. You earn a good living with predictable income. You are able to put money aside for retirement and college funds. You have an emergency fund and insurance policies that protect you from risk.

In terms of business, it means stability and profit. Your business is consistently able to pay its employees, fund projects, and earn predictable income.

This is your foundation. From here, earning more money can become a secondary priority and it becomes possible to think about the future, your values, and what could change. You can start to ask questions about your direction, who you expect to become as a person or how your business might evolve over time. This is an exploration of your values not just today, but tomorrow. What will matter to you in the future?

For us, these questions led to a realization that we didn't value running a big company or having platinum watches. What we did value was maintaining our relationship, solving a problem for our members, working from the comfort of our home, and having a healthy lifestyle and the time to pursue what we believed would make us happy.

These goals, in the context of being business owners, were not easy to reach and we needed a way to focus our efforts on these outcomes. What helped us stay focused on being Big Enough was a set of constraints around our size, business model, timeframe, and workplace. We agreed to:

- Be the sole employees and never hire a team
- Pursue licensing and phase out custom videos
- Trade higher short-term income for long-term potential
- Work from home and never have an offsite office

These constraints became a way for us to evaluate opportunities. We could always look at a new direction and ask: *if this works, will it interfere with the constraints we designed?* If so, we could assume we were on the wrong track.

Like values, constraints are a personal choice that apply to both individuals and businesses. If you've reached a point in your life that seems Big Enough, constraints are a useful way to focus your lifestyle on what matters to you. Below I've included strategies and constraints that may help get you started.

PERSONAL

- Limit social activities to two nights per week
- Reserve one evening a week for a passion project
- Plan for regular family time
- Reduce spending on specific activities like dining out
- Consider new jobs only within a twenty-minute commute
- Request to work from home when possible

BUSINESS

- Limit product lines
- Focus on limited and specific markets
- Cap the number of concurrent customers
- Reserve windows of time for specific projects
- Choose not to take outside investment money
- Limit working weeks to forty hours and make them flexible
- Reduce number of meetings
- No work on Fridays

Again, the idea of Big Enough is not about rules and strategies as much as perspective. Everyone is different and I don't want you to get caught up in the details. However, I do want to share a few tactics that may help you get started.

Once you've considered your values, gotten your financial house in order, and thought through constraints, you can start to take action. This is where the challenge really begins. Your success will depend on your fortitude and commitment to change.

As you approach this phase, I want you to feel the power of being in control. You are a revolutionary; a disrupter. You've been to the front lines and battled the forces that take your time and expect you to always want the bigger house and better car. And now, you can see that those forces have no power over you. You've found a better way and you are in control and working toward what will make you happy.

Part of that power is a willingness to say "no." This simple word is essential because it's how you wield your new power and stay in control. It's the shield that protects you from incursions into your time and lifestyle. Unfortunately, it's also very difficult to say because it often means disappointing a colleague, friend, or business partner.

It could mean saying no to a team or manager who wants you to stay at work after normal hours when you've promised to attend a dance recital. It could mean saying no to a rushed timeline so you can be sure a new product has been tested. It could mean saying no to a new consulting contract because your current projects are keeping you busy. It could even mean blocking out hours of your calendar to preemptively say no to whatever takes your time on a day-to-day basis. It could also mean removing a disruptive or toxic person from your life.

It's not easy. I'm generally a friendly person who values making a good impression and it was hard for me to say no on a regular basis. When we started seeing consistent demand for custom videos, I said no almost every day and, over time, it started to feel more natural and less rude. What helped me was learning to say no along with a logical or logistical reason why. Most of the time, our production calendar was already full, or we were focusing purely on original videos. It's never personal. We would if we could.

Of course, it's not enough to constrain your options and say no. Those are important steps and provide a means for staying in control, but they are not where the potential lives. Changing your lifestyle is like starting a creative project. You can plan and research and debate it. You can have meetings and create presentations. But in the end, what matters is starting in whatever form you can. Circumstance is an amazing teacher and if you're serious about change, you can start learning today. Make a to-do list and start checking things off. Remember that time and expenses are within your control. You can decide to change, starting right now.

It can help to be open about your plans with friends and partners. I think of it like trying to quit smoking or eat more healthily. People around you may notice that you're taking a different approach and wonder why. By sharing your vision of what's possible, you'll be able to educate them and become more committed yourself. Once you share your plans with others, you have more incentives to see them through. Peer pressure works in wondrous ways.

Big Enough is different for everyone and relates to values and having a solid financial foundation. With values as your guide, you can start to consider what it would take to live a different lifestyle that reflects the person you want to become.

Acknowledgments

I WOULD LIKE TO thank, first and foremost, my and Sachi's parents. They instilled in us an entrepreneurial spirit and a belief that we could do anything we set our minds to.

To simply acknowledge Sachi's role at Common Craft and in the book's creation is not enough. She is the heart of all we do and prefers to remain behind the scenes. I can't imagine working with anyone smarter or more thoughtful.

This book and Common Craft are possible because of our members. Their continued support and trust mean that we can keep creating videos and cut-outs that help them learn and educate others.

This book evolved significantly over time and we are fortunate to have friends and family who provided feedback along the way. Thanks to Tony Wright, Casey LeFever, Daniel Mabe, Kerry Murphy, and Anastasia Fuller. Ryan Turner and Sharon Eiler introduced me to the term "monetorium," and I'll always be grateful to them for sharing it.

I feel fortunate to have worked with the team at Page Two Books who helped me develop, design, and publish *Big Enough*. My editor at Page Two, Amanda Lewis, played a transformational role and was a constant source of encouragement and positivity.

Notes

CHAPTER 2: RETURN ON LUCK

p. 14   How much of your success do you attribute to luck versus... Gary Keller, "Are You Feeling Lucky? How Successful Entrepreneurs View Luck," *The One Thing*, https://www.the1thing.com/blog/the-one-thing/are-you-feeling-lucky-how-successful-entrepreneurs-view-luck/

p. 14   I have this thesis that the world runs on luck... Guy Raz, "Instagram: Kevin Systrom & Mike Krieger," *How I Built This with Guy Raz*, https://www.npr.org/2018/01/02/562887933/instagram-kevin-systrom-mike-krieger

p. 14   I think luck only happens when you are actively... Guy Raz, "Celebrity Chef: José Andrés," *How I Built This with Guy Raz*, https://www.npr.org/2016/11/14/501487330/celebrity-chef-jos-andr-s

p. 14   Jim Collins and Morten T. Hansen share results of a nine-year study of what they call "10X" companies... Jim Collins and Morten T. Hansen, *Great by Choice: Uncertainty, Chaos, and Luck—Why Some Thrive Despite Them All* (New York: Harper Business, 2011).

p. 15   Getting a high ROL requires throwing yourself at the luck event... Jim Collins and Morten T. Hansen, "What's Luck Got to Do with It?" *New York Times*, https://www.nytimes.com/2011/10/30/business/luck-is-just-the-spark-for-business-giants.html

p. 18   This is you, and here are your favorite websites... "RSS in Plain English," YouTube video, 3:44, April 23, 2007, https://www.youtube.com/watch?v=0klgLsSxGsU

p. 20   We decided to make another video... "Wikis in Plain English," YouTube video, 3:52, May 29, 2007, https://www.youtube.com/watch?v=-dnLooTdmLY

p. 22   Warren Buffett said, regarding his own luck... Joe Weisenthal, "We
        Love What Warren Buffet Says about Life, Luck and Winning the
        'Ovarian Lottery,'" *Business Insider*, https://www.businessinsider.com/
        warren-buffett-on-the-ovarian-lottery-2013-12

CHAPTER 3: WORK FOR HIRE

p. 26   That video is called "Google Docs in Plain English"... "Google Docs in
        Plain English," YouTube video, 2:50, September 10, 2007, https://
        www.youtube.com/watch?v=eRqUE6IHTEA&T=1s

p. 27   The video was "Twitter in Plain English"... "Twitter in Plain English,"
        YouTube video, 2:24, March 5, 2008, https://www.youtube.com/
        watch?v=ddo9idmaxoo. About 10 million viewers watched the video
        here: https://dotsub.com/view/665bdod5-a9f4-4a07-9d9e-b31ba9
        26ca78

p. 27   One of the videos that people remember most from that era... "Zombies
        in Plain English," YouTube video, 3:00, October 23, 2007, https://
        www.youtube.com/watch?v=bVnfyradcPY

p. 32   The basic idea is that companies have a choice in which markets...
        W. Chan Kim and Renée Mauborgne, *Blue Ocean Strategy: How to Cre-
        ate Uncontested Market Space and Make the Competition Irrelevant*
        (Boston: Harvard Business Review Press, 2015).

CHAPTER 4: CHOICE AS A SHAREHOLDER VALUE

p. 38   In a podcast interview with Tyler Cowen... Tyler Cowen, "Daniel
        Kahneman on Cutting through the Noise (Ep. 56: Live at Mason),"
        Conversations with Tyler, https://medium.com/conversations-with
        -tyler/tyler-cowen-daniel-kahneman-economics-bias-noise
        -167275de691f

p. 41   As one would expect, increasing income decreases negative emotions...
        David Clingingsmith, "Negative Emotions, Income, and Welfare:
        Causal Estimates from the PSID," *Journal of Economic Behavior &
        Organization* 130 (2016): 1–19, https://doi.org/10.1016/j.jebo.2016
        .07.004

p. 41   Timothy Ferriss called this the "deferred life"... Timothy Ferriss, *The
        4-Hour Workweek: Escape 9–5, Live Anywhere, and Join the New Rich*
        (New York: Crown Publishers, 2007).

p. 41   Although wealth offers the potential for people... Ashley V. Whillans
        and Elizabeth W. Dunn, "Valuing Time over Money Predicts Hap-
        piness after a Major Life Transition: A Pre-registered Longitudinal

Study of Graduating Students" (working paper 19-048, Harvard Business
School, Boston, 2018), https://www.hbs.edu/faculty/Publication%20
Files/19-048_a3814174-e598-46af-ae70-0c81cdffdb9e.pdf

CHAPTER 5: THE BUSINESS OF PERMISSION

p. 47 They wanted to show "Social Media in Plain English" in classrooms...
"Social Media in Plain English," YouTube video, 3:44, May 28, 2008,
https://www.youtube.com/watch?v=MpioclxijPE

p. 47 They wanted to upload "Social Networking in Plain English" to an intranet...
"Social Networking in Plain English," YouTube video, 1:48, June 27, 2007,
https://www.youtube.com/watch?v=6a_KF7TYKVc

p. 50 What I realized was that when I got home from work, I stopped thinking
about work... "Instacart: Apoorva Mehta," *How I Built This with Guy
Raz*, http://one.npr.org/?sharedMediaId=523003162:523047374

CHAPTER 6: DESIGNING FOR THE FUTURE

p. 55 I have all my life been considering distant effects... Witold Rybczynski, *A
Clearing in the Distance: Frederick Law Olmsted and America in the 19th
Century* (New York: Scribner, 2000).

CHAPTER 7: A PLATFORM OF ONE'S OWN

p. 64 I and the most passionate creators on YouTube... John Green, "I Don't
Care How Many People Watch Something I Make. I Care How Many
People Love What I Make," *HuffPost*, https://www.huffpost.com/entry/
communities-brandcast_b_7190140

p. 64 They created a service called Subbable in 2013... Alex Pham,
"Patreon Acquires Subbable, Aligning the YouTube Stars," *Forbes*,
https://www.forbes.com/sites/alexpham/2015/03/16/patreon-acquires
-subbable-aligning-youtube-stars/#27b2d82389f5

p. 67 like our video on Net Neutrality... "Net Neutrality—Explained by Common
Craft," YouTube video, 3:19, December 2, 2014, https://www.youtube
.com/watch?v=q0NloyxJhOk

CHAPTER 8: LIVE THE MONETORIUM

p. 87 Ramit Sethi explains the idea of conscious spending... Ramit Sethi, *I Will
Teach You to Be Rich: No Guilt. No Excuses. No BS. Just a 6-Week Program
That Works*, revised edition (New York: Workman Publishing, 2019).

p. 88   In his book *Sapiens*, Yuval Noah Harari says that many scholars see our set point of happiness... Yuval Noah Harari, *Sapiens: A Brief History of Humankind* (New York: Harper, 2015).

p. 88   Sonja Lyubomirsky, Kennon Sheldon, and David Schkade set out to find the source of "Chronic Happiness"... Sonja Lyubomirsky, Kennon M. Sheldon, and David Schkade, "Pursuing Happiness: The Architecture of Sustainable Change," *Review of General Psychology* 9(2) (2005): 111–131, https://doi.org/10.1037/1089-2680.9.2.111

p. 89   To answer this question, we can look to the work of Martin E.P. Seligman... Martin Seligman, "The History of Happiness," *The Pursuit of Happiness*, https://www.pursuit-of-happiness.org/history-of-happiness/martin-seligman-psychology/

CHAPTER 9: TURNING COPYCATS INTO CUSTOMERS

p. 94   Teaching people doesn't subtract value from what you do... Austin Kleon, *Show Your Work! 10 Ways to Share Your Creativity and Get Discovered* (New York: Workman Publishing, 2014).

CHAPTER 10: SUCCESS THROUGH FAILURE

p. 106   Shikhar Ghosh at Harvard found that 75 percent of companies with venture capital funding never return... Shikhar Ghosh's research is summarized in Faisal Hoque, "Why Most Venture-Backed Companies Fail," *Fast Company*, https://www.fastcompany.com/3003827/why-most-venture-backed-companies-fail

CHAPTER 11: THE POWER NOT TO CARE

p. 119   A famous anecdote from Greek history is the story... Plutarch, "The Life of Alexander," *The Parallel Lives*, Loeb Classical Library Edition Vol. VII (Boston: Harvard University Press, 1919), also available at http://penelope.uchicago.edu/Thayer/E/Roman/Texts/Plutarch/Lives/Alexander*/3.html#14

p. 120   I would define power as the ability to make other people... Tim Kreider, "Power? No, Thanks, I'm Good," *New York Times*, https://www.nytimes.com/2019/05/21/opinion/power-is-overrated.html

p. 122   It smells of a members-only club... Jason Fried and David Heinemeier Hansson, *Rework* (London: Vermilion, 2010).

p. 122   Are you running the business for yourself or... Matt D'Avella, "A Min-
         imalist Approach to Business," YouTube video, 18:03, June 4, 2019,
         https://www.youtube.com/watch?v=lzfuPslRRHW

p. 125   I wish I'd had the courage to live a life true to myself... Bronnie Ware,
         "Top Five Regrets of the Dying," *The Guardian*, https://www.theguard
         ian.com/lifeandstyle/2012/feb/01/top-five-regrets-of-the-dying

About the Author

LEE LEFEVER IS the co-founder of Common Craft and author of *The Art of Explanation*. Since 2007, Common Craft has won numerous awards; worked with respected brands like LEGO, Google, Intel, and Ford; and created original explainer videos that have earned over 50 million views. Today, Common Craft produces educational guides, ready-made videos, and digital visuals that are used by educators in over fifty countries. Lee and his partner, Sachi, are Common Craft's only employees and work from their home off the coast of Washington State.

WWW.LEELEFEVER.COM

HOPE YOU ENJOYED *Big Enough*. Like so much of what we do, this book was an experiment and an expression of the independence we've sought for so long. It was self-published, which means we're personally invested in its success.

I hope you'll consider reviewing it online or simply telling a friend. By sharing a few words on book review websites or where you purchased it, you can help more people discover the book and feel the satisfaction of knowing you've helped an independent publisher.

The home of my writing is leelefever.com and I'm @leelefever on social media. I'd love to hear from you! Of course, our videos and ongoing business experiments can be found at commoncraft.com.

Again, thanks so much for reading *Big Enough*!